Learning Microsoft Windows Server 2012 Dynamic Access Control

Take control of securing sensitive information whilst learning about architecture and functionality

Jochen Nickel

[PACKT] PUBLISHING enterprise
professional expertise distilled

BIRMINGHAM - MUMBAI

Learning Microsoft Windows Server 2012 Dynamic Access Control

First published: December 2013

Production Reference: 1191213

Published by Packt Publishing Ltd.
Livery Place
35 Livery Street
Birmingham B3 2PB, UK.

ISBN 978-1-78217-818-7

www.packtpub.com

Cover Image by Aniket Sawant (aniket_sawant_photography@hotmail.com)

Credits

Author
Jochen Nickel

Reviewers
Marin Frankovic
Khaled Laz
Dario Liguori

Acquisition Editor
Kevin Colaco

Commissioning Editor
Priyanka S.

Technical Editors
Menza Mathew
Rahul U. Nair
Nachiket Vartak

Copy Editors
Roshni Banerjee
Sarang Chari
Karuna Narayanan
Kirti Pai
Shambhavi Pai
Alfida Paiva

Project Coordinator
Sageer Parkar

Proofreaders
Maria Gould
Paul Hindle

Indexer
Priya Subramani

Production Coordinator
Shantanu Zagade

Cover Work
Shantanu Zagade

About the Author

Jochen Nickel is an Identity and Access Management Solution Architect working for inovit GmbH in Switzerland, and every day he tries to understand new business needs of his customers, to provide better, more comfortable, and more flexible Microsoft Identity and Access Management Solutions.

He has been working on a lot of projects, proof of concepts, reviews, and workshops in this field of technology. Furthermore, he is a Microsoft V-TSP Security, Identity and Access Management, Microsoft Switzerland, and uses his experience for the directly managed business accounts in Switzerland. He has also been an established speaker at many technology conferences.

Jochen is very focused on Dynamic Access Control, Direct Access, Forefront UAG/TMG, ADFS, Web Application Proxy, AD RMS, and the Forefront Identity Manager. Committed to continuous learning, he holds Microsoft certifications such as MCT, MCSE/A, MCTS, MTA, and many other security titles. He enjoys spending as much time as possible with his family to get back the energy to handle such interesting technologies.

For more information about *Microsoft Windows Server 2012 Dynamic Access Control*, you can visit my blog at `http://blog.idam.ch`.

Thanks to my dear colleagues from Microsoft and my business partner for supporting me and helping me to handle this great technology. Also, thanks to my lovely family for giving me the time to realize such projects.

About the Reviewers

Marin Frankovic was born in Makarska in 1976, where he completed his elementary schooling and part of high school. He graduated from high school in the USA, where he attended his senior year as an exchange student. In 2003, he earned a Mag. oec. degree from Faculty of Economics, Zagreb, majoring in Business Computing. As a student, he volunteered in the faculty's IT department for a year as technical support. After obtaining his degree, Marin started as a Microsoft MOC and an IBM ACE instructor in the largest private IT education company, Algebra. There, he also started as a consultant for infrastructure, virtualization, and cloud computing based on Microsoft technologies. Later on, when Algebra opened a private college for Applied Computing, he took on the position of Head of the Operating Systems department, and undertook the responsibility of creating the course curriculums and managing several lecturers and assistants. He also does lectures on several key courses in the system administration track. For five years in a row, Microsoft honored him with an MVP title for System Center and Datacenter Management. Marin is a regular speaker on all regional conferences, such as Windays, KulenDayz, MobilityDay, NT Konferenca, MS Network, DevArena, and so on. In 2011, he was awarded the Microsoft ISV award for his contribution to the Microsoft community. Marin regularly writes technical articles for IT magazine *Mreža*. His main interests today are cloud computing, virtualization as its core component, and resource consolidation based on Microsoft technologies, such as Windows Server and System Center applications.

Khaled Laz is an IT professional working for CCC, the largest construction company in the Middle East.

His experience focuses on troubleshooting and maintenance of IT networks. He holds more than a dozen certificates in the IT field, such as CCNA, MCITP, MCSE, MCSA, and many others.

Together with his extensive experience, he is a qualified expert in the area of System and Network Administration.

Dario Liguori is an MCTIP, MCSE, MCT, CCNA Security, VCP, Network+, Server+, and ITIL certified professional. He has over 20 years of experience as an IT consultant/trainer. He started working in the IT field using MS-DOS and Windows 1.01.

Over the years, his experience has covered a broad range of products, including NetWare, Lotus Domino, Windows NT, Exchange Server, IIS, Proxy Server, and so on.

He currently works for one of the most important Microsoft UC Gold Partners in Italy and the UAE as a senior consultant.

He has been involved in a wide range of projects in several countries for medium/large organizations.

Dario's primary focus is design and delivery of Microsoft infrastructure (SCCM, SCOM, SCVMM, TMG, SQL, Lync, Exchange, Hyper-V, AD DS, AD CS, AD FS, AD RMS, RDS, Cluster, NLB, Office 365, and so on).

Table of Contents

Preface

In today's complex IT environments, file servers play an increasingly important role, storing tons of data and information and making it available to any individual in an organization. Additionally, all of this data needs to be secure and accessible across varied networks, devices, and applications and needs to enact with strategies like **Bring Your Own Device** (**BYOD**), Direct Access, and the different cloud scenarios.

For system administrators, this starts quite often with building groups for controlling access to the company's internal file servers. For example, Jack works on a project called Ikarus and he needs some information from the Marketing department, but Jack is not really a member of that department. Therefore, you are going to build some security groups to solve this request and a complex group scenario starts to exist. Since the groups and their memberships will grow and in each case become more and more complex; just think about the Kerberos token bloat, which brings problems of user authentication.

In addition, it is always a challenge to audit and monitor solutions. You might be familiar with situations such as "Who had access to the sensitive finance information on June 1, 2013?" or the wonderful "Access denied" message that leads a user to come to you to ask you for access to a particular information. Or, immediately you will start searching to provide the **Chief Information Security Officer** (**CISO**) of the organization with the right information for evidence or who is the owner of this information to decide whether to give the user the proper access or not.

Furthermore, a common challenge is to decide how to provide infrastructure or services on a cloud. The main reason is that the companies don't really know what information is sensitive and what is not. Classifying the information helps in this case and can allow different cloud scenarios.

Dynamic Access Control (**DAC**) is a complete end-to-end solution to secure information access and not just another single new feature of the Windows Server 2012. DAC can really help you to solve some daily problems you may face in giving access to data on distributed file servers. These are a few points that we will discuss in this book:

- Classify your information
- Define and implement Access Control Policies based on classification
- Define and implement Central Audit Policies
- Provide additional information protection with Rights Management Services

Dynamic Access Control is the right tool to use if you need control over the data level so that the data stay with the files even if they are leaving the file server. Furthermore, DAC is useful if you care about many attributes, and you need device information for the authorization process in your own or a partner Active Directory forest—at least if you need an automated process to classify information based on attributes or resource properties.

What this book covers

Chapter 1, Getting in Touch with Dynamic Access Control, will cover the business needs, purposes, and benefits of Dynamic Access Control. We will discuss and study the architecture in detail and start by building the test lab and our first simple solution.

Chapter 2, Understanding the Claims-based Access Model, will explain the idea of identities and claims especially in the use of Windows 8 and Windows Server 2012. It will also suggest how Kerberos Armoring and Compound Authentication works and about how to manage claims and resource properties. The test lab will guide you deeper into the functionality of DAC.

Chapter 3, Classification and the File Classification Infrastructure, will review the required information to map the business and security requirements to classify information. We will also explain the different methods to classify information and how the File Classification Infrastructure and the Data Classification Toolkit can support your implementation.

Chapter 4, Access Control in Action, will focus on Central Access Policies. The Central Access Policies are one of the most important components, and we will explain how to define, configure, and manage them with a staging and productive environment. The chapter will also discuss access-denied assistance.

Chapter 5, Auditing a DAC Solution, will cover the usage of conditional expressions and the global object access auditing settings and options that System Center Suite provides you with to build an efficient and comprehensible solution.

Chapter 6, Integrating Rights Management Protection, will discuss the important aspects of the Active Directory Rights Management Services integration in a complete information protection context.

Chapter 7, Extending the DAC Base Solution, will cover methods and tools to get the necessary data quality in Active Directory for using Dynamic Access Control. We will also provide an overview of important third-party tools, SharePoint, and Bring Your Own Device strategy integration.

Chapter 8, Automating the Solution, will cover the automation possibilities such as the Forefront Identity Manager, System Center Suite, and Data Classification Toolkit for Dynamic Access Control. The chapter also gives you an idea of different architectures to fulfill the different requirements in actual projects.

Chapter 9, Troubleshooting, will discuss common problems and how to address them. It gives you a tutorial from the general to the advanced troubleshooting strategies for Dynamic Access Control. The chapter will also offer a collection of external resources such as blogs, wikis, and articles.

What you need for this book

You will need at least a Windows 2012 R1 or R2 Domain Controller and File Server with a domain-joined Windows Client to use all the described functionality. The Windows Server Operating System is available as a trial or licensed version, and you can download it from the Microsoft download center or from the public website of Microsoft. Additionally, if you want to extend the solution, you will need System Center Suite, Forefront Identity Manager, Data Classification Tool, and Security Compliance Manager.

Who this book is for

This book is intended for IT consultants/architects, system engineers, system administrators, and security engineers who are planning to implement Dynamic Access Control in their organization or have already implemented it and want to discover more about its abilities and how to use them effectively. To use the book efficiently, you should have some understanding of security solutions, Active Directory, access privileges / rights, and authentication methods. Programming knowledge is not required but can be helpful for using PowerShell or the APIs to customize your solution. Advanced automation and development of extensions are not in the scope of this book. The book also requires a fundamental understanding of Microsoft technologies.

Conventions

In this book, you will find a number of styles of text that distinguish between different kinds of information. Here are some examples of these styles, and an explanation of their meaning.

Code words in text, database table names, folder names, filenames, file extensions, pathnames, dummy URLs, user input, and Twitter handles are shown as follows: "You can also use the command `gpudate /force`, which forces the computer to update its group policy right away."

Any PowerShell input or output is written as follows:

```
Set-ADUser -CompoundIdentitySupported:$true or $false
```

New terms and **important words** are shown in bold. Words that you see on the screen, in menus or dialog boxes for example, appear in the text like this: "Follow the wizard and click on **Work Folders** under **File and Storage Services** | **File and iSCSI Services**."

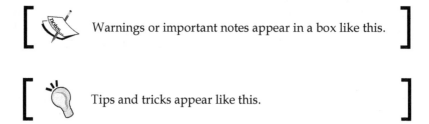

Warnings or important notes appear in a box like this.

Tips and tricks appear like this.

Reader feedback

Feedback from our readers is always welcome. Let us know what you think about this book—what you liked or may have disliked. Reader feedback is important for us to develop titles that you really get the most out of.

To send us general feedback, simply send an e-mail to `feedback@packtpub.com`, and mention the book title via the subject of your message.

If there is a topic that you have expertise in and you are interested in either writing or contributing to a book, see our author guide on `www.packtpub.com/authors`.

Customer support

Now that you are the proud owner of a Packt book, we have a number of things to help you to get the most from your purchase.

Errata

Although we have taken every care to ensure the accuracy of our content, mistakes do happen. If you find a mistake in one of our books—maybe a mistake in the text or the code—we would be grateful if you would report this to us. By doing so, you can save other readers from frustration and help us improve subsequent versions of this book. If you find any errata, please report them by visiting `http://www.packtpub.com/submit-errata`, selecting your book, clicking on the **errata submission form** link, and entering the details of your errata. Once your errata are verified, your submission will be accepted and the errata will be uploaded on our website, or added to any list of existing errata, under the Errata section of that title. Any existing errata can be viewed by selecting your title from `http://www.packtpub.com/support`.

Piracy

Piracy of copyright material on the Internet is an ongoing problem across all media. At Packt, we take the protection of our copyright and licenses very seriously. If you come across any illegal copies of our works, in any form, on the Internet, please provide us with the location address or website name immediately so that we can pursue a remedy.

Please contact us at `copyright@packtpub.com` with a link to the suspected pirated material.

We appreciate your help in protecting our authors, and our ability to bring you valuable content.

Questions

You can contact us at `questions@packtpub.com` if you are having a problem with any aspect of the book, and we will do our best to address it.

1
Getting in Touch with Dynamic Access Control

Dynamic Access Control (**DAC**) is a complete, end-to-end solution to secure information access and is not just another new feature of Windows Server 2012. DAC can really help you to solve some daily problems you may have in giving access to data on distributed file servers. For example, Jack works on a project called **Ikarus**, and he needs some information from the marketing department, but Jack is not really a member of that department. Therefore, you are going to build some security groups to solve this request, and a complex group scenario starts to exist, because the groups and their memberships will grow and in each case become more and more complex. In addition, it is always a challenge to audit and monitor such a solution. You might know situations such as "Who had access to the sensitive finance information on June 1, 2013?" Or the wonderful "access denied" message a user encounters that leads them to ask for access to a particular piece of information. Immediately you start searching to provide the Chief Information Security Officer (CISO) of the organization the right information for evidence on who the owner of this information is for the CISO or the data owner to decide whether or not to give the user proper access. These are a few short examples that we will discuss in the following chapters to give you a broad overview. Do not forget that we will go in deep in the following chapters.

The topics we will cover in this chapter are:

- Business needs, purpose, and benefits
- Inside the architecture of DAC
- Building your smart test lab
- Getting started with your first real-life solution

Business needs, purpose, and benefits

In today's complex IT environments, file servers play an increasingly vital role. We store tonnes of data and information on them, which is distributed for many individuals in an organization. Additionally all of this data needs to be secure, accessible across varied networks, devices, and applications, and needs to enact with strategies like **Bring Your Own Device** (BYOD), **Direct Access**, and different **Cloud** solutions.

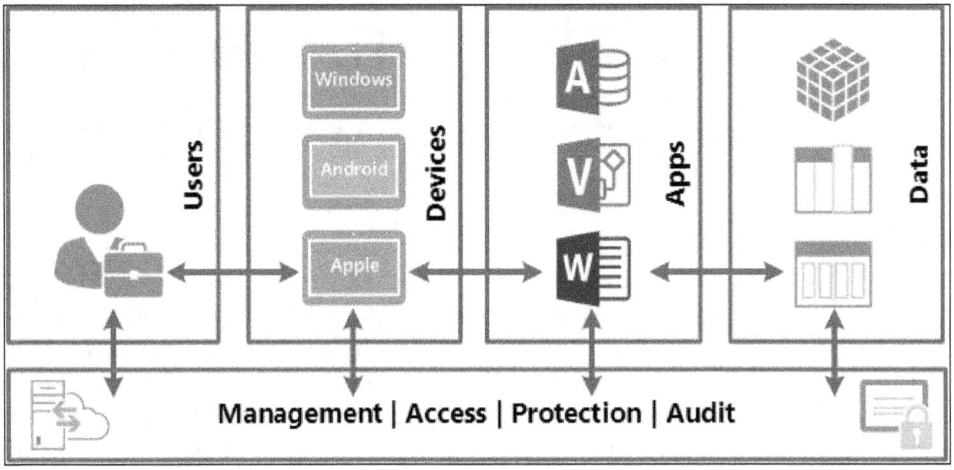

To hold the costs down while meeting the security requirements is always a challenge for those responsible.

The main challenges for data owners or file server administrators are as follows:

- The numbering and management of security groups needs to be reduced as illustrated in the simple example consisting of the **Account – Global Groups – Domain Local Groups – Permissions** principles shown in the following diagram:

> A new acronym from Microsoft can also be used:
> **IGDPA**: Identities, global groups, domain local groups, access

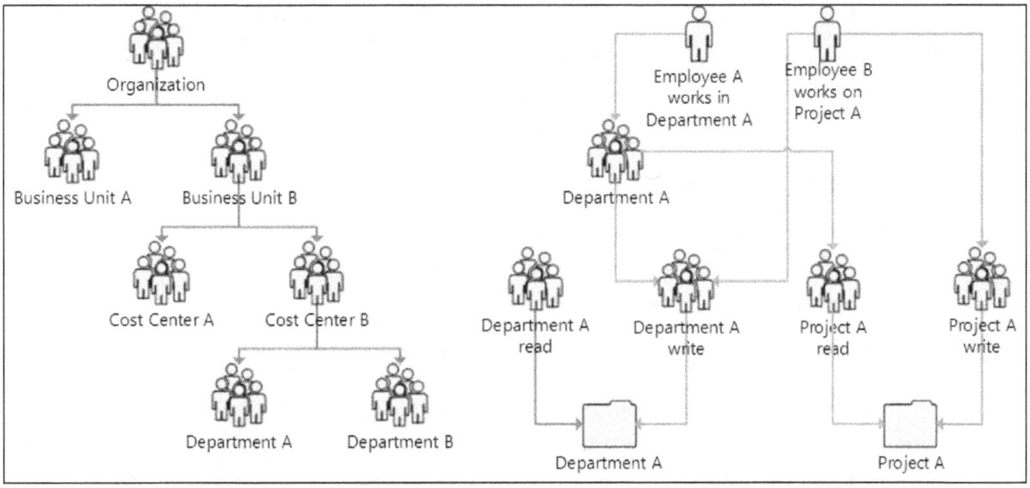

The idea of the following list is to show a part of the current challenges with respect to managing, securing, and maintaining information. Feel free to extend the list infinitely for your notes:

- Central access and audit management of business and compliance needs
- Building enhanced authentication and authorization scenarios (for example, BYOD)
- Sensitive information needs to be protected wherever it goes
- The productivity of information workers should not be affected
- The content owners should be responsible for their information
- To provide access-denied assistance messages to provide a managed end-to-end scenario

So the million-dollar question is, "How can **Dynamic Access Control** help you to address and solve these requirements?".

Dynamic Access Control provides you with the following enhanced ways to control and manage access in your distributed file server environment:

- Classification: Identify and classify your information based on their content. There are four ways to tag information; by location, manually, automatically, and using application APIs.
- Control access: Build up the precise definitions of the right person, with the right permission, at the right time, from the defined device. Usage of the **Central Access Policy** (**CAP**) will help you to address the following common security policies, compliance (general, organization-wide, departmental, specific-data) and the need-to-know principle.

- Compliance: This is a response to governmental regulations, but it can also be a response to industrial or organizational requirements:
    - U.S. Health Insurance Portability and Accountability Act (HIPPA)
    - Sarbanes-Oxley Act (SOX)
    - U.S. data breach laws
    - Basel I/II/III, U.S.-EU Safe Harbor Framework, EU Data Protection Directive
    - PCI, NIST SP 800-53/122
    - Japanese Personal Information Protection Act
- Policy staging: This allows you to control changes to CAPs by comparing current settings against new settings by firing event log entries into the system log. Information can be analyzed using Event Viewer or by connecting with System Center Operations Manager.
- Access denied remediation: In current environments, you get just a very simple access-denied message, which is not very helpful for the helpdesk or the user. DAC provides additional information and the opportunity to send information that is more useful to the data owner.

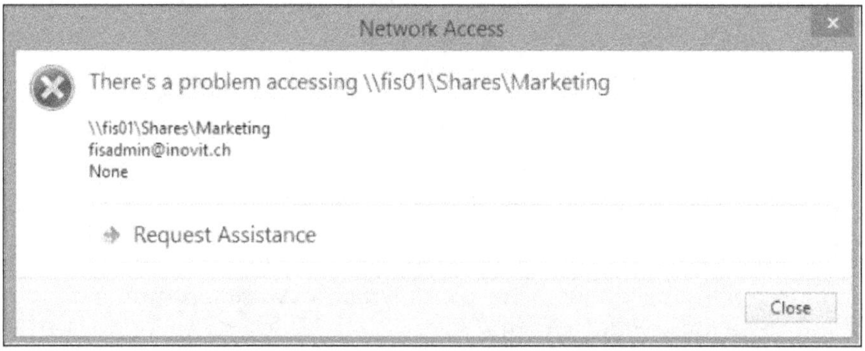

- Audit: Defining policies based on information security, organizational and departmental requirements for reporting, analysis, and forensic investigation. Central Audit Policies form the key answer provided by Dynamic Access Control for those requirements.
- Protection: Dynamic Access Control integrates with **Active Directory Rights Management Services** (**AD RMS**) for classification-based automatic encryption of sensitive tagged information. This option helps in any transmission aspect to protect the content against any unauthorized person.

Now that you have had a little recap about the business needs, the purpose, and the benefits of Windows 2012 Dynamic Access Control, we can dive into the technical details.

Inside the architecture of DAC

As promised in the previous section, Dynamic Access Control is not just a single feature, but an end-to-end file server solution based on the following features in Windows Server 2012:

- Windows authorization and audit engine supporting expression-based access control
- Kerberos version 5 support for user and device claims
- File classification infrastructure that supports claims
- RMS support that can be extended for further file types from third-party vendors
- API to extend the solution with custom classification and audit tools

Building blocks

The Dynamic Access Control solution can be logically divided into the following main components to get a better, granular overview:

- Infrastructure requirements
- User and device claims
- Expression-based ACEs
- Classification enhancements
- Central access and audit policies
- Access-denied assistance

These different building blocks are explained in the following sections with all the details. But first, you need to get a quick overview of the most important facts of Dynamic Access Control. We will start the overview with the infrastructure requirements.

Infrastructure requirements

For basic deployment of Dynamic Access Control, you do not need to put in a big effort. To use claims for authorization and auditing, there is only a need for the following components:

- At least one Windows 2012 or newer domain controller
- Configure DAC objects, which are:
  - **Claim Types**
  - **Central Access Rules**
  - **Central Access Policies**
- Administering with **Active Directory Administrative Center** (**ADAC**) or **Remote Server Administration Tools** (**RSAT**) installed on Windows 8/ Windows Server 2012 or newer

> A Claim is something that Active Directory states about a specific object (user or computer). A Claim may include the user, a unique **Security Identifier** (**SID**), department classification of a file or other attributes of a file, user, or computer.

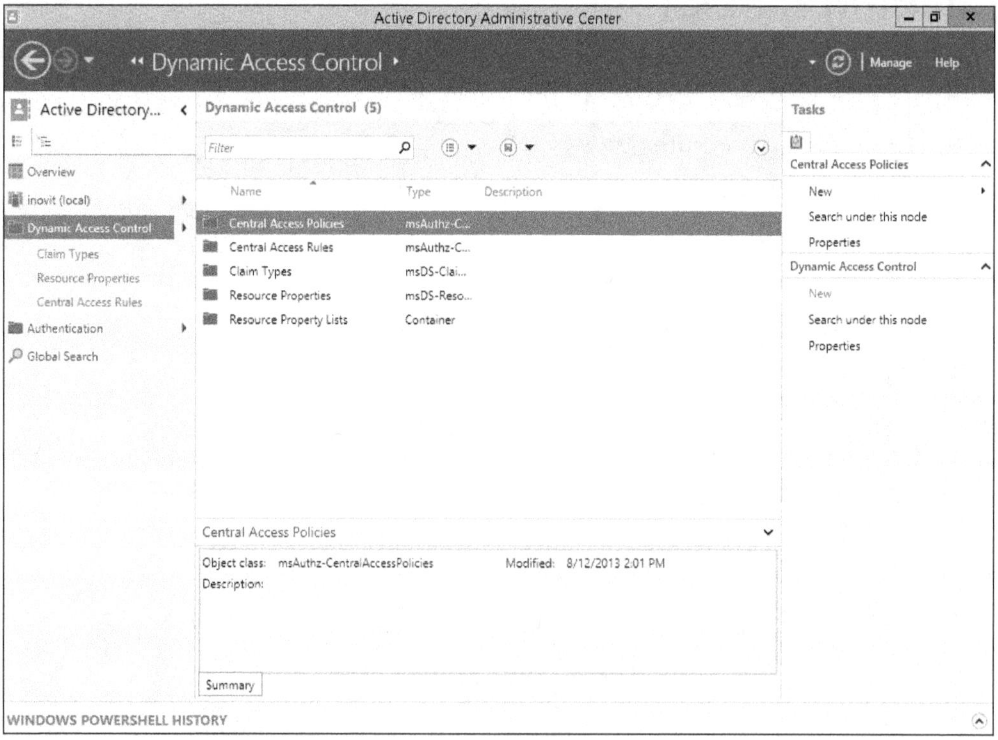

- Group policy to deploy Central Access Policies to your file servers
- Group policy to enable the KDC support for claims
- Group policy to enable the Kerberos client support for claims
- All the file servers that use DAC must be 2012 or newer
- Windows 8 or newer client computers must be part of that domain (only required when using device claims)
- AD RMS role must be enabled and configured if you want to use automatic encryption
- You need to enable claims support on domain controllers and clients (disabled by default)
- DAC stores all configurations in the Active Directory configuration partition
- Group policies are used to configure DAC on file servers and clients
- The **File Server Resource Manager** (**FSRM**) brings up many features such as **File Server Classification Infrastructure** (**FCI**)
- Dynamic Access Control also works over organization boundaries with **Claims Transformation Policies** (**CTP**)

The following figure shows the basic deployment and configuration that needs to be done

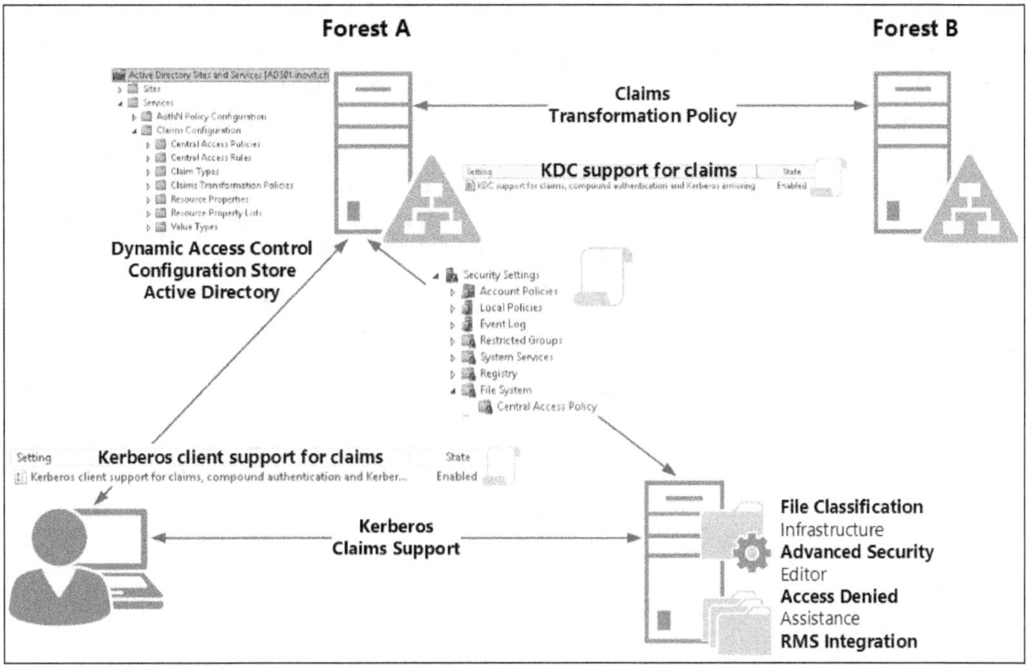

However, what happens if you don't use Windows 8 clients?

> For non-Windows 8 / Windows Server 2012, such as XP, Vista or Windows 7, the user doesn't need to worry about claims. In that case, the 2012-based file server will query the Active Directory services and forward the claims request to get information about the claims the user or the machine provides.

As you can see in the figure above, DAC works between different **Active Directory Forests** (Active Directory instance of an organization), and Claims Transformation Policies will provide the functionality to translate the claims definitions between two or more organizations. To prepare for this scenario, you need to establish a **Forest Trust** between the **Active Directory Forests** and the **Domain Function Level (DFL)**, which in both the Forest Root domains must be Windows 2012 or higher. Right now, this is a challenge but also a necessary requirement. There is no need for Claim Transformation Rules inside a Forest. This works fine out of the box because Dynamic Access Control objects are stored in the configuration part of the Active Directory and the whole Forest knows the relevant information.

User and device claims

Traditionally, you may have secured access to files by using NTFS file permissions and security groups. With this configuration, we were restricted to making policy decisions based on the user's group membership and the number of groups will explode. Therefore, if we wanted to include the device to control access, there was no chance to do this in an earlier version of the Windows Server. Another limitation was the requirement for folder or file access based on a certificate. Before Windows 2012 Dynamic Access Control, there was no way for the built-in functionality to include devices or certificates. DAC now integrates claims into Windows Authentication so that we can use Active Directory attributes from users and computers to control access to our information stored on file servers such as a location, department, or project.

> DAC will only be used as complementary technology and is not a replacement for security groups.

The following figure shows the new combinations you can use for authorization:

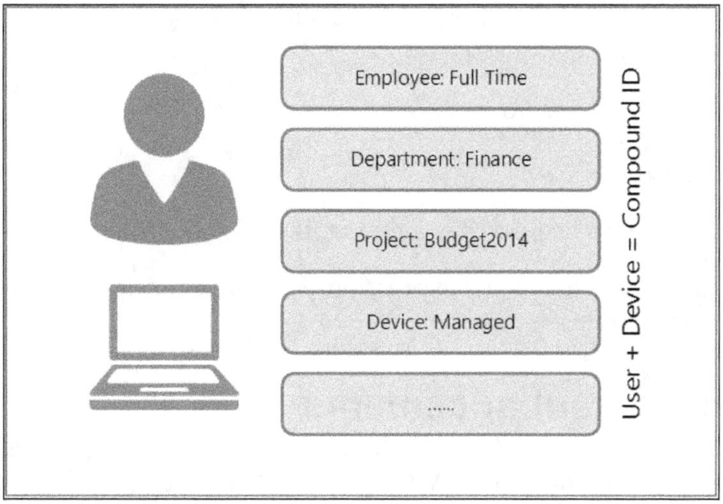

This opens new ways of giving permissions on files and folders, such as:

```
Allow | Read, Write |
If (@User.Department == @File.Department)
AND (@Device.Managed == True)
```

> There is no development knowledge required to implement a Dynamic Access Control solution.

Expression-based access rules

By using expression-based access control, users or devices must satisfy conditions that we define to access files in a given classification.

To explain the major benefits, we use a very easy and common example. Let us consider that 200 projects, 20 countries, and two divisions are part of an organization. So in fact, this results in something like 8,000 groups to solve the access control in this scenario using the traditional approach. Reducing security groups is always a vital task in the current IT environment. For example:

- Project Budget2014 CH Finance Users
- Project Budget2014 UK Finance Users

Windows Server 2012, without claims, already allows multiple groups with a Boolean logic (expression-based Access Control lists). This helps us to reduce the groups in an effective way. Let us look at the following example of using the `AND` operations to build up a permission model:

```
Allow Modify IF MemberOf(ProjectA)
AND MemberOf(CH)
AND MemberOf(Finance)
```

The result is 222 groups instead of something like 8,000 security groups. Yeah!

Finally, by using claims inside the expression-based access rules, we can convert the groups into exactly three user claims.

Classification enhancements

The first task in every Dynamic Access Control project is to identify and classify files based on their content. With Windows 2008 R2, we could already fulfil the following tasks:

- Define classification properties
- Automatically classify files based on location and content
- Apply file management tasks (file expiration / custom commands) based on classification
- Produce reports

With Windows Server 2012, the following classification improvements are added:

- Manual classification (Windows Explorer)
- Continuous classification (File Server Resource Manager)
- Folder-based inherited classification
- Conditional access control entries (additional authorization layer)

The next figure gives you an introduction to the processes carried out in a file classification scenario and shows the continuous classification:

1. Define resource properties in Active Directory such as a department or company, and apply them to your file servers.
2. The File Classification Infrastructure checks the file content and classifies the information with the correct classification.
3. After classifying the information, the classification can be used for authorizing access to the information.

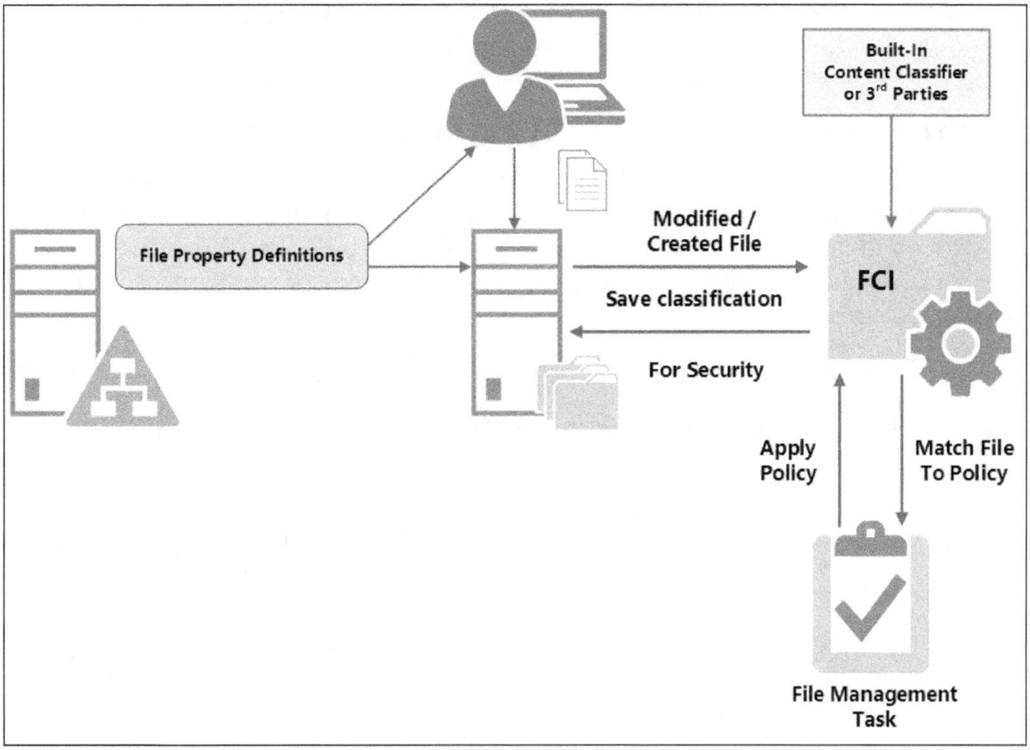

With the Windows Server 2012 File Classification Infrastructure (FCI) feature, you can identify sensitive files and encrypt them automatically with RMS.

Some possible scenarios include:

- Access to all documents on the file server must be limited to active, full-time employees of the company—even if an employee distributes copies to different places, such as **Skydrive**, **Dropbox**, or **SharePoint**
- The AD RMS-policy of **Finance read only** must be applied to all files containing more than 10 credit card numbers or other Personal Identifiable Information (PII)
- The AD RMS-policy of **Sales Managers only** to all Excel files larger than 100 MB containing **Personal Identifiable Information** (**PII**) and 10 contract numbers being created by the CRM system

This technology also gives you the possibility of supporting file types other than Office documents. You just need to install and configure a combination of FCI with **Rights Protected Folder Explorer** from `http://blogs.technet.com/b/rms/archive/2012/06/29/official-release-of-rights-protected-folder-explorer.aspx`.

Otherwise, you need to add a third-party solution to provide support for other file types.

Central Access and Audit policies

Central Access Policies (CAPs) play an essential role in a Dynamic Access Control scenario. CAPs are a set of authorization policies that we manage in the Active Directory and deploy them to the file servers over Group Policies. You can think about a CAP-like safety net policy to give you another idea of what you can expect from that element.

A CAP has two logical parts:

- Defined conditions as to which files the policy will be applied
- List of one or more Access Control Entries (ACEs)

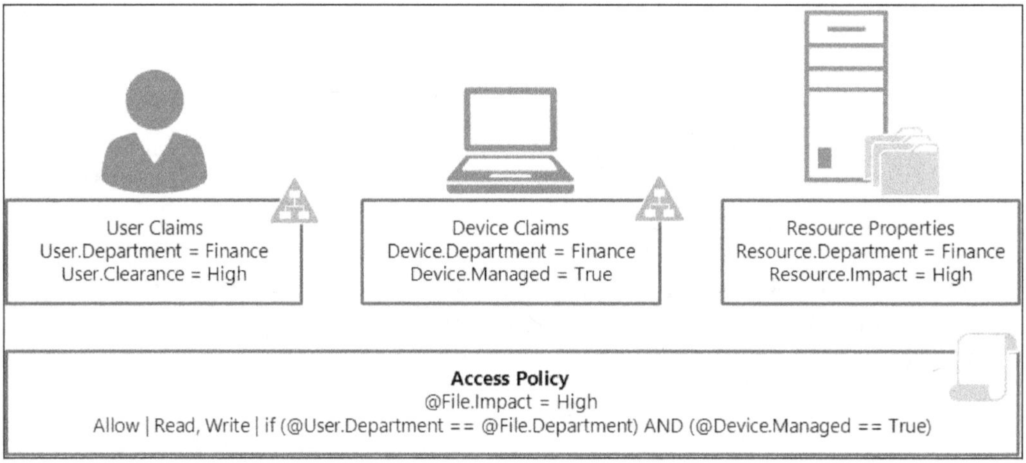

The next figure should provide you with some information on how the different solution components interact and where the information of the DAC objects is stored. Furthermore, it gives you the necessary tasks in the right order and the tools that you can use to configure CAPs, claims, and property definitions.

Obviously, if you change policy, you want to check the consequences of your work. For this reason there is a function called "policy staging" available, which lets you run a new policy parallel to your current configuration to evaluate the results.

On the left-hand side of the following figure, you see the tasks that need to be done to configure Dynamic Access Control, and on the right-hand side, the results on the system.

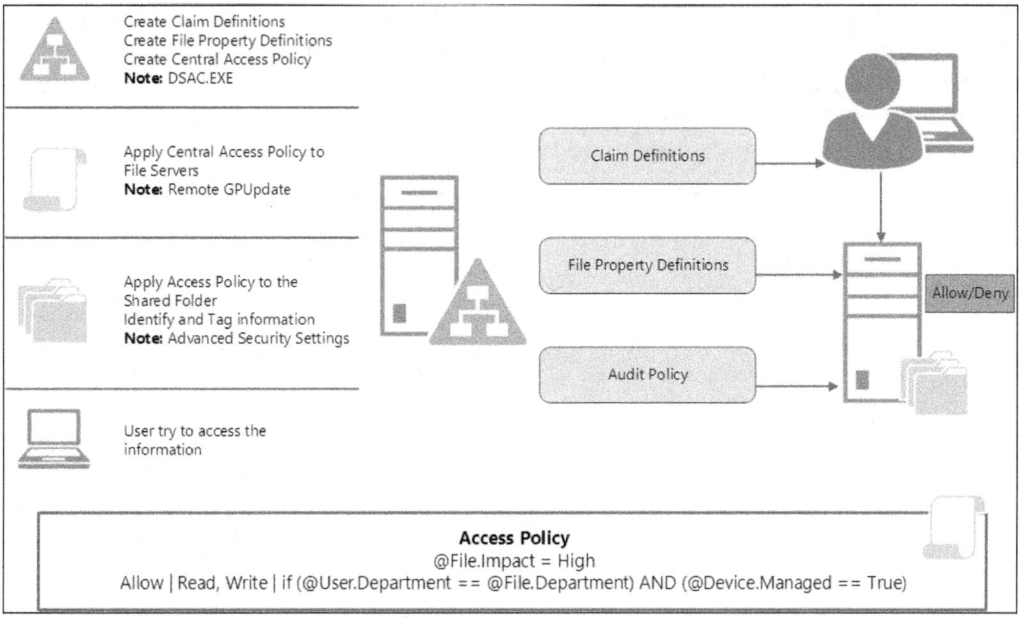

Also, a new tab is present in the **Advanced Security Setting for Finance Documents** called **Central Policy**.

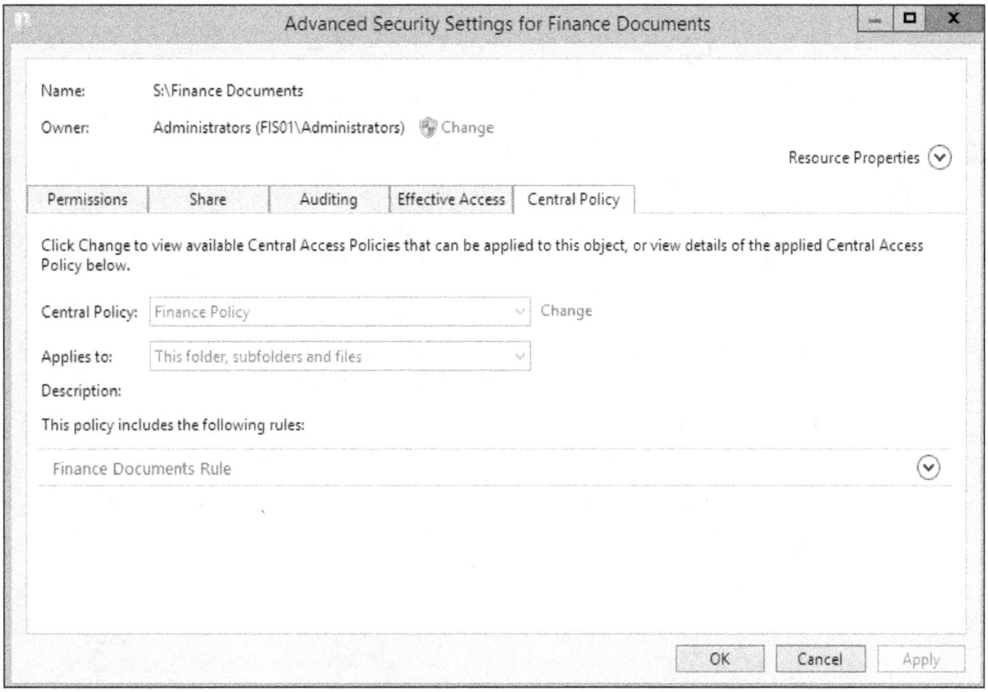

After applying Central Access Policies, we need to think about Auditing Policies. With Windows Server 2012, you can author audit policies by combining claims and resource properties. It enables scenarios for you that were impossible or very hard to implement until now. The next figure shows you the file-access auditing workflow to give you a better understanding of this process:

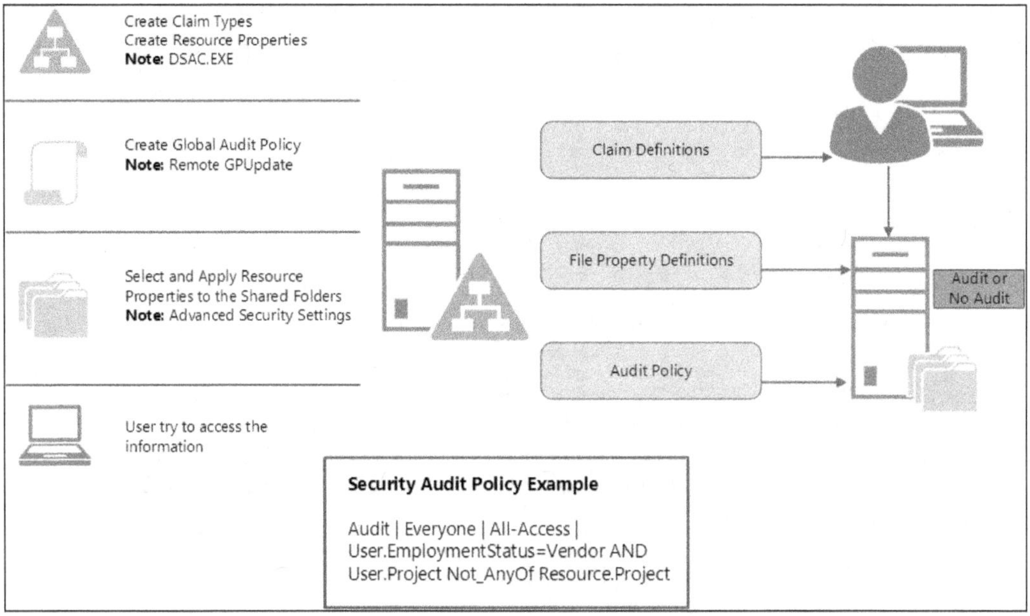

A quick look at how much power is inside these new audit improvements:

> Auditing everyone who is not working on a specific project and trying to access information tagged as only accessible for full-time employees and a project member working on that project is now possible.

To view and analyze audit events you can use the common Event Viewer or if available, the System Center Operations Manager with the Audit Collection Service configured.

Access-denied assistance

Access-denied assistance is a role service of the File and Storage Services role in Windows Server 2012 and helps us in the following use cases:

- Users get more than just an Access-denied message. They are provided with detailed information for the data owner, helpdesk, or file server administrators.
- Allows user to request access from the data owner.

There are two ways to configure the Access-denied assistance:

- E-mail - The user gets a customized access-denied message with a button to request assistance and an e-mail fired to the data owner
- Web service - The user gets a customized access-denied message with a link included and gets redirected to a self-service portal, such as Forefront Identity Manager 2010 R2

> The minimum requirement to use access-denied assistance is at least a Windows 8/Windows server 2012/8 RT or newer devices.

Building your smart test lab

While building our smart and straightforward test lab, we will start to apply our knowledge in a practical way. Not wanting to spend hours, we start with a minimal lab and extend it step-by-step for our needs.

We start with the following configuration:

- A domain controller Windows 2012 R2 (build your own Forest, such as `inovit.ch`)
- A domain-joined File Server Windows 2012 R2
- A domain-joined Client Computer Windows 8.1 Pro

You might have noticed that we are using the latest versions. IT professionals always like to touch the newest one! In fact, we need this version because in further labs, we will show you how to integrate Dynamic Access Control in a Bring Your Own Device scenario including a Work Folders configuration.

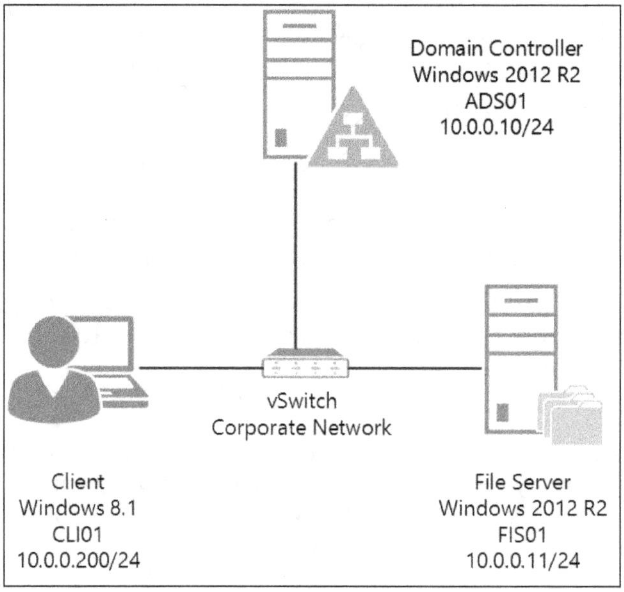

There are no special requirements on the virtual environment, such as disk, CPU, or memory configuration. Just use your common configurations. Feel free to start as well with the Base Windows 2012 R2 Test Lab Guide at `http://www.microsoft.com/en-us/download/details.aspx?id=39638`.

On the file server, add an additional virtual disk to provide **Shared Folders** for our little test company and create a file structure as follows:

1. Create a shared folder for each country (`CH`, `FR`,and `MA`).
2. Additionally, create a folder for each office location (`Zurich`, `Paris`, `Rabat`, and `Casablanca`).
3. Additionally, create a folder for each department (`Sales`, `Human Resources`, `Engineering`, `Marketing`, and `Help Desk`).
4. Under the department folders, create a folder called `Sensitive`.
5. The structure looks like **MA | Casablanca | Marketing | Sensitive**.

6. Create a shared folder for some example projects (Project A, Project B, Project C).
7. Create a shared folder for some public information.

Configuring Dynamic Access Control

The next steps will provide you with the main tasks to implement your first Dynamic Access Control configuration.

Create some test users in your Active Directory with a minimum of 10 users and:

1. Define the Active Directory claim types.
2. `Country`, `Department`, and `Location` for the folder structure decided earlier.
3. Populate the three attributes for the 10 test users.
4. Define the Resource properties for `Country`, `Department`, and `Location`.
5. Define the Active Directory Access Rule as follows:

```
(Resource.Country equals User.Country) AND
  (Resource.Location equals User.Location) AND
  (Resource.Department equals User.Department)
```

6. Build a Central Access Policy and deploy the Access Rule to the file servers.
7. Build a Resource Property list, and deploy it to the file servers.
8. Open an administrative PowerShell, and fire `gpupdate /force` and `Update-FSRMClassificationPropertyDefinition` on the file server.
9. On the resources, apply the Resource properties correctly.

> Every folder gets a `Country`, `Department`, and `Location` stamp.

10. Apply the Central Access Policy to the file shares.
11. Apply the Access Rule to *all* the `Country` shares and the `Location` and `Department` folders.
12. Try out whether access is allowed or not.

Try to fix this first short solution with the help of the provided information on this chapter or use the following lab to give you some advice to solve this problem:

`http://online.holsystems.com/Software/holLaunchPadOnline/holLaunchPadOnline.application?eng=TENA2013&auth=none&src=CommNet&altadd=true&labid=8697`

Summary

This chapter introduced a lot of new concepts and information such as the business needs, purpose, and benefits and the main components of Dynamic Access Control. It is always important to get a general overview of a technology to get a better understanding about the scope of what we need to go through. Don't worry if it sounds like you will get many things to study, for after understanding the main principles, you will see a successful deployment of Dynamic Access Control very soon.

2
Understanding the Claims-based Access Model

This chapter will explain the idea of identities and claims especially in the use of Windows 8 / Windows Server 2012 and higher. This chapter will also define how Kerberos Armoring and Compound Authentication works and how to manage claims and resource properties. Test lab will guide you to go deeper into the functionality of **Dynamic Access Control** (**DAC**). In this chapter you will learn about:

- Understanding claims
- Windows 8/ Windows Server 2012 and newer claims support
- Kerberos Armoring and Compound Authentication
- Managing claims and resource properties
- Using Claim Transformation and Filtering
- Groups or DAC, let's extend our first solution

By the end of this chapter you will have learned what a claim is and how to work with it. Furthermore, you will have configured a first advanced solution in the lab environment. The solution provides you an understanding about when to use groups or claims for authorization. Also, the situation in which a combination of both can help you to fulfill your requirements in configuring access control to your information stored on a file server.

Understanding claims

Before we define what a claim is, we need to talk about identities. We can say that **identity** is a set of information that can uniquely identify anything and contains information about the subject's relationships to other entities. Identities, in general, are verified by using a trusted source of information. We can say a digital identity is a set of information to identify a person.

Now that we have defined the term **identity**, we can discuss a few examples about claims in the real and technical world. In general, claims are statements about an identity:

- **Passport**: It is a common example; if you want to fly, you need to show your passport that contains information such as your name, address, date of birth, and a biometric photo. Each item is a claim made about you by the country issuing your passport. Your country ensures that the information in your passport is correct and can be trusted by other countries.
- **Bartender**: In theory, he should check if you are of the required minimum age before serving alcohol. The only claim he is interested in is your age and the document is checked by him.
- **Certification authority**: Digital certificates include claims such as the subject, certificate thumbprint, or a distinguished name, and the certificate gets verified by a trusted certificate authority.
- **Active Directory**: In this, claims are statements about a specific object such as a user or computer. Some examples are the user's department, his title, or whether the computer is managed or not.

Before Windows Server 2012, it was only possible to authenticate and authorize with **Security Identifier** (**SID**), and security groups that represented the identity of a user or a computer used in **Access Control Entry** (**ACE**). Windows Server 2012 extends this limitation with the support of conditional expressions. Now you can use user claims and device claims for file and folder authorization in addition to NTFS permissions based on users' or groups' SIDs.

With Dynamic Access Control, we can use three types of claims:

- **User claims**: It provides information about a user
- **Device claims**: It provides information about a computer
- **Transformation claims**: It is used in claim transformation policies to transform the claims exiting or entering a trusted forest

An issued claim has three characteristics or properties and needs to be conformed with the following syntax:

- The claim identifier must start with `ad://ext/` and must be unique
- Up to 32 characters may follow the claim identifier
- The 32 characters may not contain spaces, \, *, ?, ", <, >, and |
- It cannot end with a forward slash (/)

Property	Value
Type	ad://ext/company/1
Value	inovit
Value type	string

> Claims will not be issued by default. You need to configure this functionality in Kerberos **Key Distribution Center** (**KDC**) on your domain controllers, and the Kerberos client support for Windows authorization claims.

The following screenshot shows the default behavior on a client:

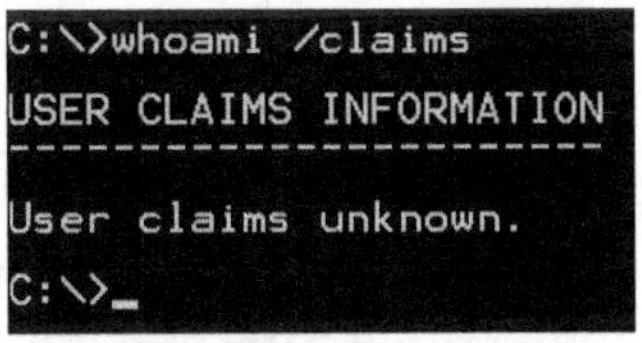

On the domain controller you can check the configuration of the krbtgt account:

- Claims are not used with **msDS-SupportedEncryptionTypes** set to **0x0 = ( )** as shown in the following screenshot:

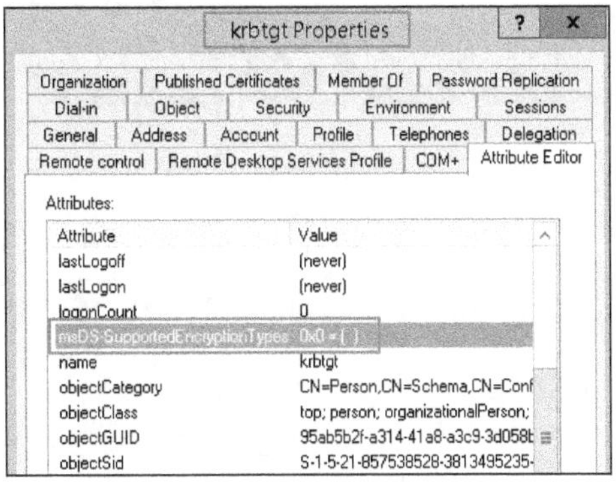

- Claims will be used with **msDS-SupportedEncryptionTypes** set to **0x50000 = (0x50000)**

To enable claims support you need to create at least two group policies with some standard settings. On your domain controller, a policy with the following settings needs to be applied:

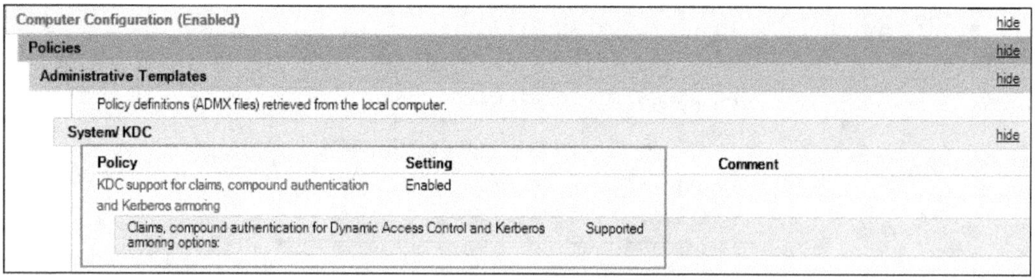

On your client computer, a policy with the following settings needs to be applied:

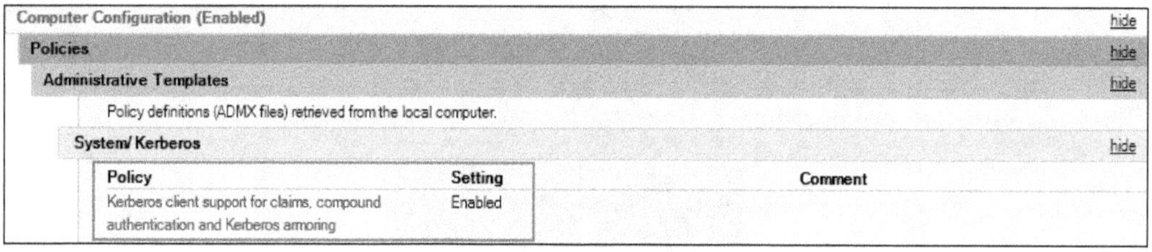

Use `gpupdate/force` to refresh your Group Policy settings on your domain controller and your client computer, to test the functionality immediately.

By configuring the first claim type in **Active Directory Administrative Center** and populating the **Department** attribute for the user in Active Directory, we receive our first result as shown in the following screenshot:

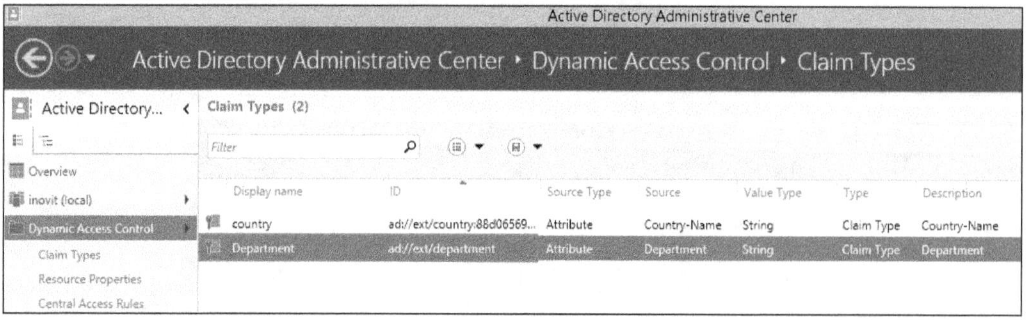

The result on the user side looks like the following screenshot:

```
C:\Users\jleano>whoami /claims

USER CLAIMS INFORMATION
-----------------------

Claim Name   Claim ID                Flags Type   Values
============ ======================= ===== ====== =========
"Department" ad://ext/department           String "Finance"

C:\Users\jleano>
```

The following default data types for claims are valid:

- **Boolean**: It is a true/false integer-based data type
- **Multi-valued String**: These are one or more string values
- **Multi-valued Unsigned Integer**: These are one or more positive integer values
- **Security Identifier**: These are one or more security identifiers
- **String**: These are literal alphanumeric characters
- **Unsigned Integer**: This is a positive numerical value

Claims support in Windows 8/2012 and newer

The following section gives a short introduction to the most important changes in the Kerberos protocol.

Kerberos authentication enhancements

The Kerberos authentication enhancements include:

- Kerberos **Security Support Provider (SSP)**

  The main enhancement is placed in `Kerberos.dll` that includes user claims and device authorization. This functionality helps you to use your device information for authorizing access to a file or folder.

- **Key Distribution Center** (KDC)

  KDC support claims.

- Claim information within the **Privilege Attribute Certificate** (**PAC**) includes:
    - **PAC in Pre-Windows 2012**: It contains user and group membership security identifiers
    - **PAC in Kerberos Ticket Granting Ticket** (**TGT**): It contains information for a security principal and is optional for a device
- NT Token sections

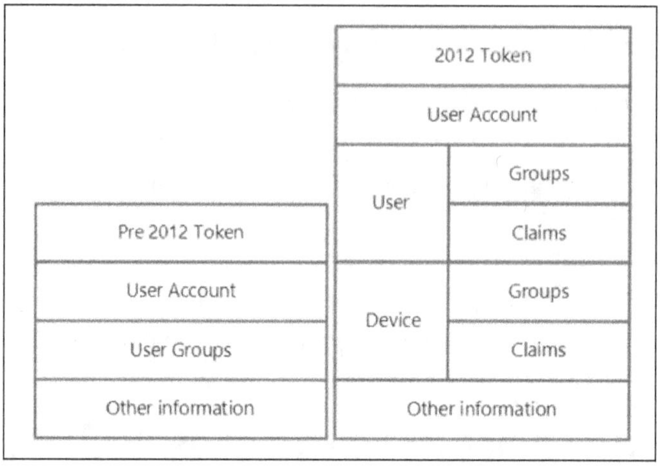

The part to the right of the preceding figure shows the new authentication token (**2012 Token**) that can be used. The main difference is that now devices and user claims can be used to authorize access to a file or folder.

- Kerberos Armoring (FAST)

  Kerberos Armoring has been officially named as **Flexible Authentication Secure Tunneling** (**FAST**) by RFC 6113.

- Compound Authentication

  Compound Authentication allows **Ticket Granting Service** (**TGS**) to include two identities, User and Device.

- Token size reduction and default maximum token size of 48 KB

  Warning events for large Kerberos tickets are placed under `Computer Configuration\Policies\Administrative Templates\Systems\KDC\`.

The maximum token size by default is 12 KB for versions till Windows 7 and Windows Server 2008 R2. If your Kerberos token becomes too large because of being a member of many groups, your users will receive error messages during login and applications that use Kerberos authentication will potentially fail.

The following figure shows the Kerberos flow in a pre-Windows 2012 file server access solution, where no claims are used in accessing a file server and traditional access controls apply.

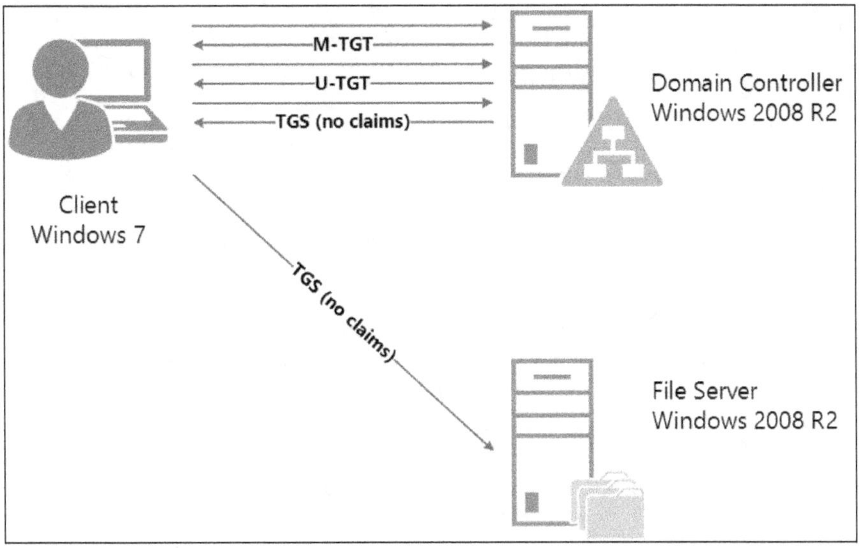

The default configuration of Windows 8 / Windows Server 2012 and newer versions work the same as in Windows 2008 R2 and Windows 7 environments. For claims support, the administrator needs to enable it by configuring group policy settings for your client machines under `Policies\Computer Configuration\Administrative Templates\System\Kerberos`.

You can define the Kerberos client support for claims, Compound Authentication, and Kerberos Armoring under `Policies\Computer Configuration\Administrative Templates\System\KDC`. KDC support for claims, Compound Authentication, and Kerberos Armoring is provided in the relevant group policy setting.

> If device claims are enabled in a Dynamic Access Control solution, Windows 8 Client or Windows Server 2012 and newer will always use Windows 2012 or newer domain controllers to request the Kerberos tickets.

The following figure shows the changed Kerberos flow with the usage of claims:

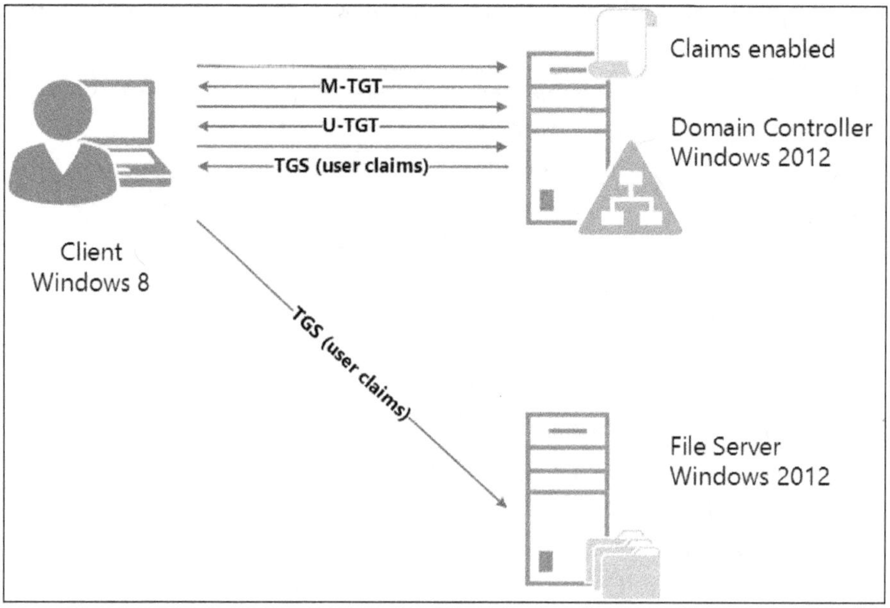

Be sure to plan enough Windows 2012 domain controllers in your Active Directory environment. Monitor the **KDC AS** (**KDC Authentication Service**) and TGS request performance counters to determine the count of domain controllers.

After claims deployment, monitor the following performance counters:

- KDC AS request with claims for domain controllers
- KDC AS requests with FAST for domain controllers
- KDC TGS requests with FAST for domain controllers

In a mixed environment, be sure to use the supported method in the group policy settings of KDC configurations for claims, Compound Authentication, and armoring to support all the legacy factors.

Furthermore, there will be no issues for your legacy clients to access file servers with the Dynamic Access Control permission, because in such a scenario the fileserver will query the Active Directory and forward the claims request to figure out which claims the users and machines have and whether your solution is working well. So the file server checks the name of the user and with that information it evaluates the access to your shared files as shown in the following screenshot:

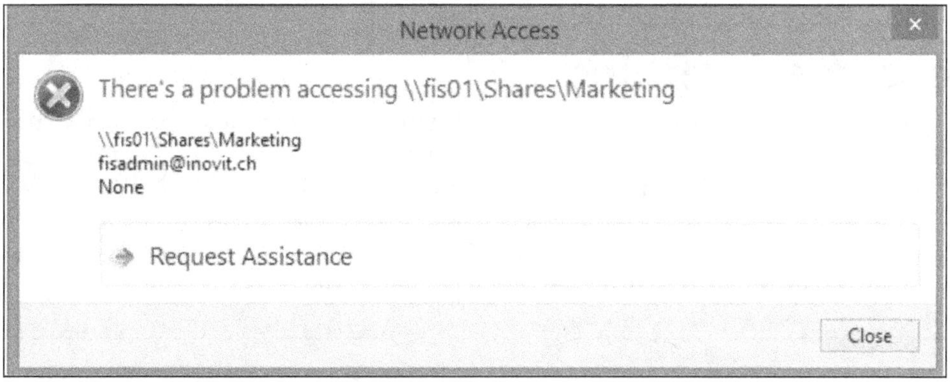

[The access-denied messages are only available on Windows 8 / Windows Server 2012 and newer versions.]

The following figure shows the changed Kerberos flow when claims are not used:

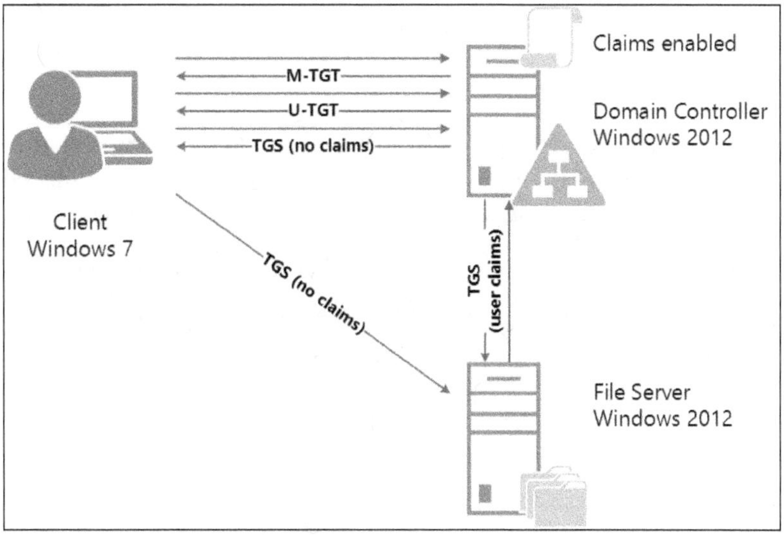

Kerberos Armoring and Compound Authentication

There are two major enhancements in the Kerberos authentication to provide a more secure Kerberos protocol and the chance to use the user and device claim for compound authentication. We will start with the Kerberos Armoring feature.

Kerberos Armoring

The **Flexible Authentication Secure Tunneling** (**FAST**) provides a protected channel between the Kerberos client and the KDC. You can see the protected channel marked with red lines in the following figure. In Windows 2012, FAST is called Kerberos Armoring and it is only available for **Authentication Service** (**AS**) and **Ticket Granting Service** (**TGS**) exchanges. The following figure gives you an idea about the conceptual architecture and the communication flow:

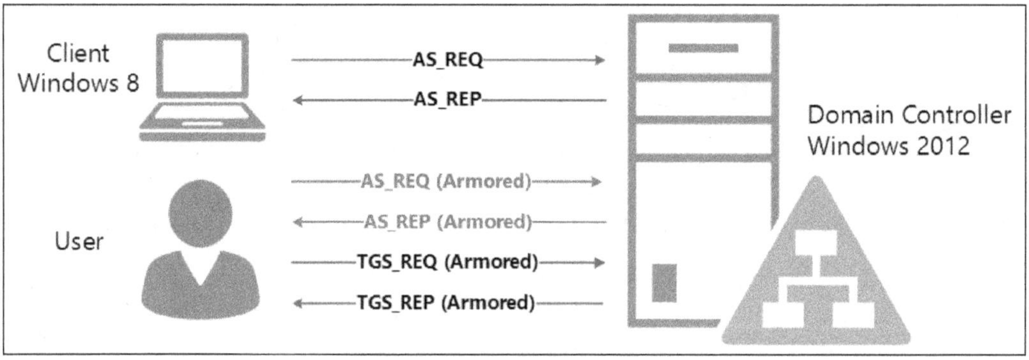

In Windows 2012, the following are the four Dynamic Access Control and Kerberos Armoring policy settings to configure the behavior of these settings, placed under `Computer Configuration\ Policies \Administrative Templates\System\KDC`:

- Do not support Dynamic Access Control and Kerberos Armoring
- Support Dynamic Access Control and Kerberos Armoring
- Always provide claims and FAST RFC behavior

- Unarmored authentication requests will fail because a protected channel is required and cannot be provided by legacy machines

> Some additional reading on the topic can be found from the following links:
>
> - `http://blogs.dirteam.com/blogs/sanderberkouwer/archive/2012/09/05/new-features-in-active-directory-domain-services-in-windows-server-2012-part-11-kerberos-armoring-fast.aspx`
> - `http://technet.microsoft.com/en-us/library/hh831747.aspx`

Compound Authentication

By default, Windows 2012/8 and higher devices can work with DAC Kerberos tickets where data needed for compound authentication is included. Compound Authentication results in an access token that includes the identity of the user and the device on resources that recognize Dynamic Access Control.

You need to enable Compound Authentication using group policy settings. There are three options in that configuration:

- **Never**: No Compound Authentication will be provided by the KDC
- **Automatic**: A DAC-aware application installed and registered itself under `HKEY_LOCAL_MACHINE\SYSTEM\CurrentControlSet\Services\Netlogon\Paramaters\CompoundIdentity`
- **Always**: Compound Authentication will be provided by the KDC

Another option is to enable/disable compound authentication separately on single objects:

- User object: For this, use the `Set-ADUser -CompoundIdentitySupported:$true` (enable) or `Set-ADUser -CompoundIdentitySupported:$false` (disable) command
- **Group-managed service accounts**: For this, use the `Set-ADServiceAccount -CompoundIdentitySupported:$true or $false` command
- **Computer Accounts**: For this, use the `Set-ADComputer -CompoundIdentitySupported:$true` (enable) or `Set-ADComputer -CompoundIdentitySupported:$false` (disable) command

The following figure shows the Kerberos flow with Compound Authentication enabled:

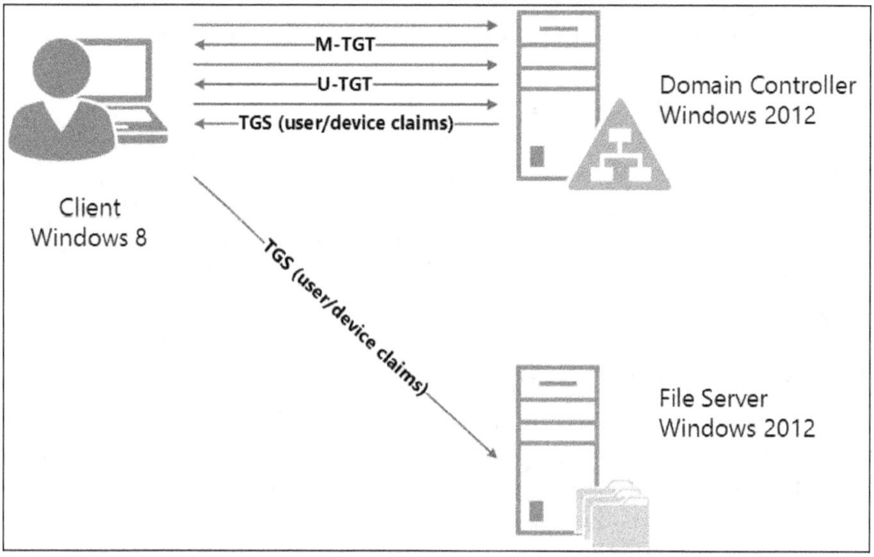

You can get more information on Kerberos from the following links:

- `http://social.technet.microsoft.com/wiki/contents/articles/4209.kerberos-survival-guide.aspx`
- `http://msdn.microsoft.com/en-us/library/windows/desktop/aa378747(v=vs.85).aspx`

Managing Claims and Resource properties

As you already know, Dynamic Access Control is not a feature that can be quickly activated because you need to handle a lot of requirements and planning before you can productively use this feature. After knowing the real business needs and regulations, you need to apply one of the important planning steps.

After the identification of the claims and resource properties, you should think about the following information, because they are used for resource access decisions.

Naming conventions

One of the first things you should be aware of is a well-designed and working naming convention for different Active Directory objects and attributes:

- **Groups**: They are **File Service + Department + Read/Write** (**FIS-HR-RW**).
- **Employee type**: It can be **FTE** (**Full Time Employee**) or Vendor.
- **Title**: It provides a list of used job titles inside your company (like Senior Developer or Principal Consultant).
- **Office**: It provides structure to the attribute (for example, CH-ZURICH-B6F2O4, Switzerland, Zurich, Building 6, Floor 2, and Office 4).
- **Location**: It defines the language you want to use for the location.
- **Claims and resource properties**: It uses clear statements and follows the strict naming context and syntax for claims and resource properties. The details about syntax for claims is present at `http://msdn.microsoft.com/en-us/library/windows/desktop/jj552963(v=vs.85).aspx` and the details about syntax for resource properties is present at `http://msdn.microsoft.com/en-us/library/windows/desktop/jj552964(v=vs.85).aspx`.

> Get organized with naming conventions. Use the opportunity to sanitize your data inside your Active Directory.
>
> The list we just mentioned is just a starter. Work on it, and you will feel happy with your Dynamic Access Control solution.

Authoritative system and data validation

It is very important to think about an authoritative system from which your Active Directory receives the correct information.

For example, you could use the HR system to provide you the information. However, be aware, we are all humans and mistakes or misspellings can happen and with Dynamic Access Control, permissions are changed immediately in the Active Directory because the authorization is based on the Active Directory attribute you would have populated using wrong values. So provide a validation script for a double approval of the information from the HR department.

The following figure shows you an example of this process to use a script with validation options to populate Active Directory attributes based on an HR export file:

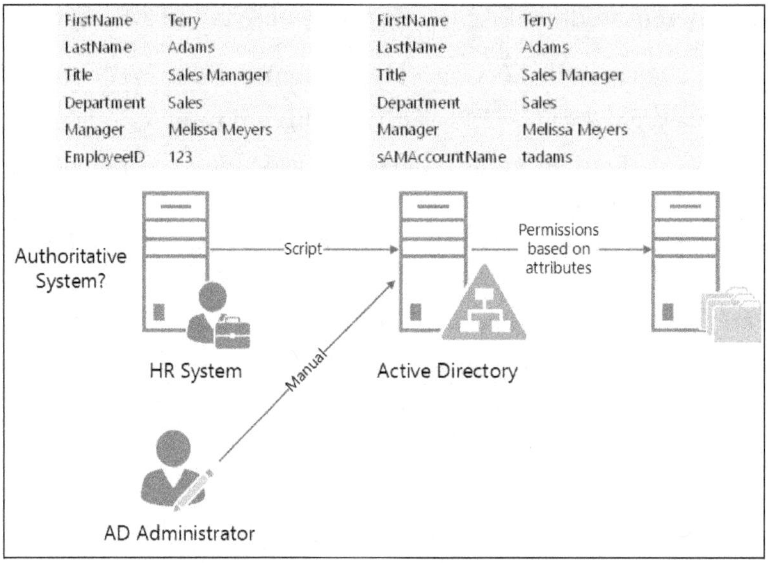

Be careful about how your script sets Active Directory attributes. Common mistakes are blank spaces inserted from scripts or by the administrators in Active Directory attributes. So see to it that your script sets the attribute to `<not set>` as shown in the following screenshot:

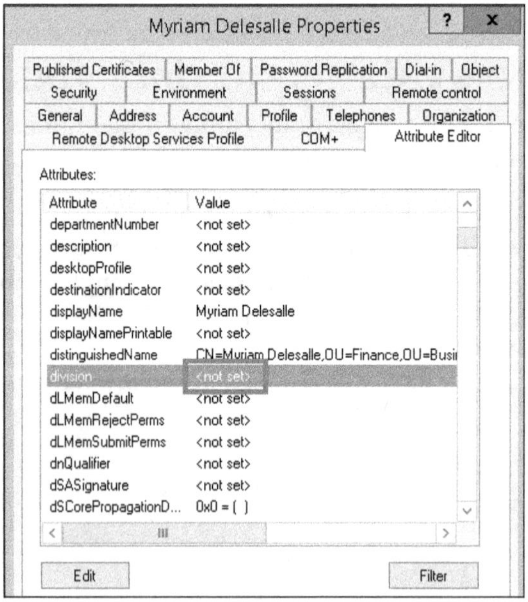

Administrative delegation

In addition, you should know who could write into the user and computer attributes, because those who have the right to do that are able to modify access decisions.

Ideally, you should delegate administrative permissions for all Dynamic Access Control containers. The following list shows you the most important administrative roles:

- DAC claim admins
- DAC resource property admins
- DAC central access rule admins
- DAC central access policy admins

The relevant containers under **Configuration** | **Services** | **Claims Configuration** are **Claim Types**, **Resource Properties**, **Central Access Rules**, and **Central Access Policies**.

The following figure shows the containers in Active Directory:

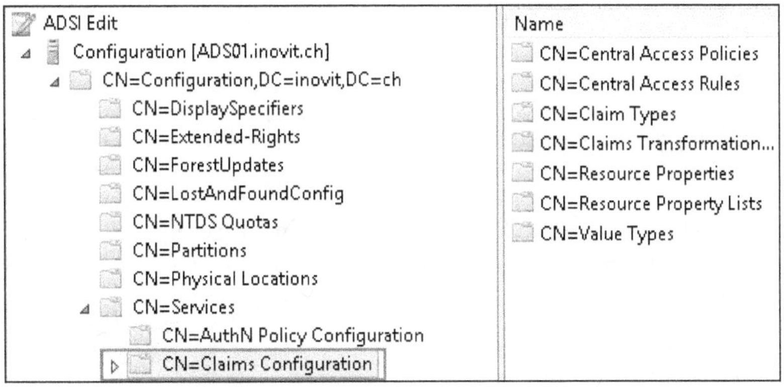

Resource properties

The value of **File Classification Infrastructure** (**FCI**) in Windows 2012 and newer is very important, because you can use resource properties for authorization decisions. Now you configure authorization access based on one or more resource property values by using conditional expressions. Resource properties, in general, use alternate data streams within each metadata for the file. One of the many properties is **Project**, because in every organization you have projects that you need to provide access to. The following figure shows the administrative console for defining the properties:

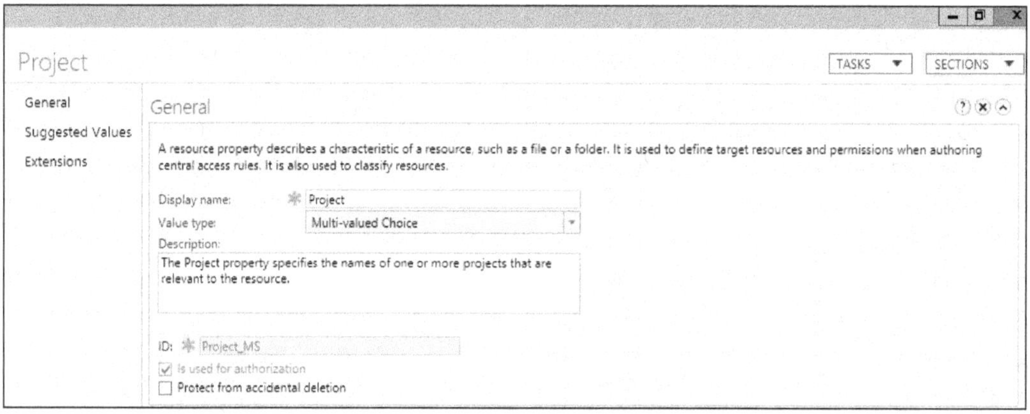

With this technology, you can solve very complex scenarios. Two resource property types are available:

- **Resource Property object**: It is a complete instance of a resource property and the suggested values for any resource property are stored in `msDS-ClaimPossibleValues`
- **Reference Resource Property object**: They do not store their own values, they reduce manual maintenance of data consistency

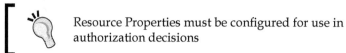

> Resource Properties must be configured for use in authorization decisions

You will see more about Resource Properties in the next chapters.

Using Claim Transformation and Filtering

If you need to work with claims over organization boundaries, you will need **Claim Transformation Policies** (**CTPs**) and Filtering; an Active Directory trust relationship is also a requirement for such a scenario. One of the important requirements that challenge organizations is that in every forest you want to use claims, a Windows 2012 **Domain Functional Level** (**DFL**) is required.

> A Windows 2012 DFL means that only Windows 2012 Domain Controller or newer is allowed to be part of the domain. You can get more information at `http://technet.microsoft.com/en-us/library/cc771294.aspx`.

In our projects we have, for example, account forests and resource forests on a green field and in such a scenario, there is normally no problem to meet that requirement. Furthermore, there is always a good chance to meet these requirements when you bring the environments on an actual Operating System level and use the other advantages of Windows 2012. The following figure introduces you to the Kerberos flow in a forest-to-forest scenario:

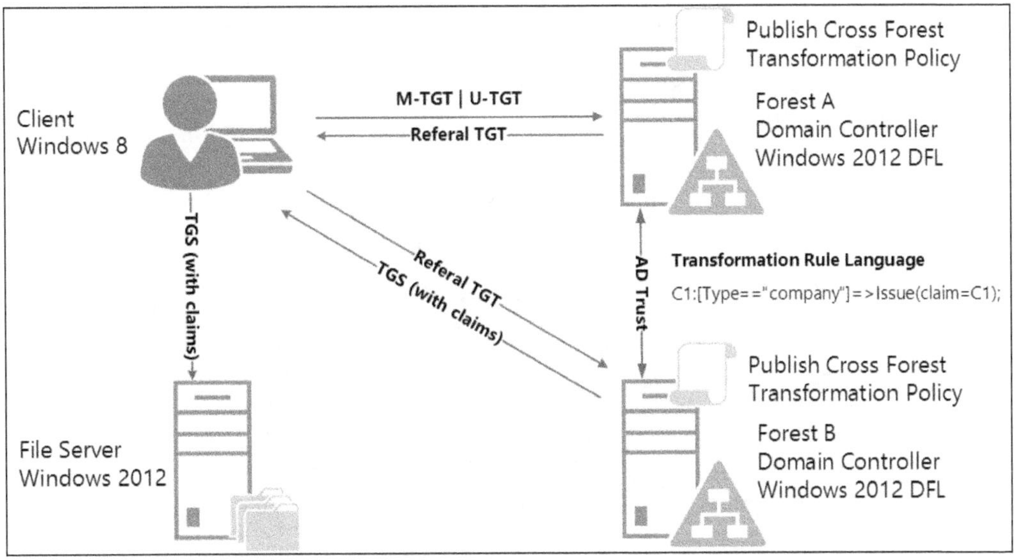

Windows 2012 and newer provides three basic scenarios for filtering and transforming claims:

- **Value-based filtering**: It allows the trusted forest to prevent claims with certain values from being sent to the trusting forest.
- **Claim type-based filtering**: It prevents Windows from sending claims that disclose information to the trusting forest.
- **Claim type-based transformation**: It uses transformations to generalize the claim type, claim value, or both.

In the next chapters, we will use some examples to go deeper into that process.

Groups or DAC, let's extend our first solution

The next lab presents you with some challenges to get you familiar with Dynamic Access Control. Try the following things based on the knowledge you already have:

Extend the lab from *Chapter 1, Getting in Touch with Dynamic Access Control*, and solve the following problem:

- First, you can use traditional group memberships as shown in the following figure.
- Second, you can use Dynamic Access Control

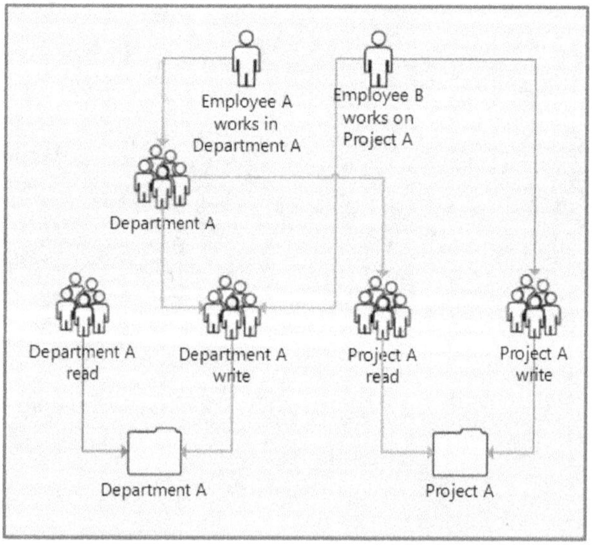

Summary

After reading this chapter you should be able to define an identity and a claim because these are the two requirements for using Dynamic Access Control. Additionally, we tried to give a very quick overview of the Kerberos enhancement in Windows Server 2012 and we recommend that you read the additional information about Kerberos provided in this chapter to get deeper knowledge. It is just impossible to put all the information about Kerberos in this book. Also, think about the main decisions for managing claims and resource properties to get the right permissions at the right time, and for the right person. In the next chapter we will discuss the purpose of classifying information and the use of the FCI.

3

Classification and the File Classification Infrastructure

Now that we have finished the first two chapters, which explained the idea of DAC, this chapter will teach you how to map the different requirements for an efficient classification solution. Next, you will be able to use the Windows File Classification Infrastructure and the Data Classification Toolkit for solving your classification requirements.

In this chapter we will be covering the following topics:

- Mapping the business and security requirements
- Identifying the different types and methods of tagging and classifying information
- Using the Windows File Classification Infrastructure
- Exploring the Data Classification Toolkit 2012
- Designing and configuring classification

After reading this chapter, you should have all of the tools and information you need for classifying your data.

Map the business and security requirements

In an organization, all forms of information, including ideas and concepts, have potential business value; for example, financial information. It is important that everyone is responsible for protecting this information. The first step to secure information is to classify it based on the impact of unintentional disclosure. For example, Microsoft uses three types of information classifications based on the impact:

- **High Business Impact** (**HBI**):
  - Could cause severe or catastrophic material loss to the information asset owner or reliant parties
  - Control access to HBI assets by the *need-to-know* principle

  Examples for this information include:

  - Unannounced financial reports
  - Personally Identifiable Information such as a social security or driver license numbers
  - Intranet site or file share
  - Credit card number, name, and expiration date
  - Medical information, PINs
  - Username and password lists
- **Moderate Business Impact** (**MBI**):
  - Could cause serious material loss to the information asset owner or reliant parties
  - Control access to the MBI assets by the business need for access

  Examples for this information could be a team status report with the employee name, current and next week activities, and planned offsite days. More examples include:

  - Criminal background information
  - Contact information (business/personal)

- **Low Business Impact (LBI)**:
    - Could cause limited or no material loss to the information asset owner or reliant parties

  A typical example could be a corporate newsletter, or information on Intranet sites or file shares.

The preceding three types of classification are found predefined in your DAC environment, and you can use them straightforwardly. If the data falls into more than one classification, use the more restrictive one. Additionally, ask your legal department how to handle this information. Always treat information as HBI if it is marked as HBI or confidential. Don't share information unless you really know that it is really LBI information, and remove the HBI and MBI information from your computer before you give it away.

Protect the HBI and MBI information using secure technologies such as the following:

- S/MIME for mail delivery
- IRM to restrict forwarding, copying, and printing
- Encryption to store the file locally, or on a shared area

[You will find more information at `http://www.microsoft.com/en-us/download/details.aspx?id=20135`.]

The following table gives you some baseline classification properties for your daily work:

Area	Properties	Values
Information Privacy	Personally Identifiable Information	High; Moderate; Low; Public; Not PII
	Protected Health Information	High; Moderate; Low
Information Security	Confidentiality	High; Moderate; Low
	Required Clearance	Restricted; Internal Use; Public
Legal	Compliancy	SOX; PCI; HIPAA/HITECH; NIST SP 800-53; NIST SP 800-122; U.S.-EU Safe Harbor Framework; GLBA; ITAR; PIPEDA; EU Data Protection Directive; Japanese Personal Information Privacy Act
	Discoverability	Privileged; Hold
	Immutable	Yes/No
	Intellectual Property	Copyright; Trade Secret; Parent Application Document; Patent Supporting Document
Records Management	Retention	Long-term; Mid-term; Short-term; Indefinite
	Retention Start Date	<Date Value>
Organizational	Impact	High; Moderate; Low
	Department	Engineering ;Legal; Human Resources ...
	Project	<Project>
	Personal Use	Yes/No

(Source: Microsoft)

Different types and methods for tagging and classifying information

Typically, there are four ways to apply tags to information in a Windows environment. With DAC, you are able to use them for your needs as shown in the following figure:

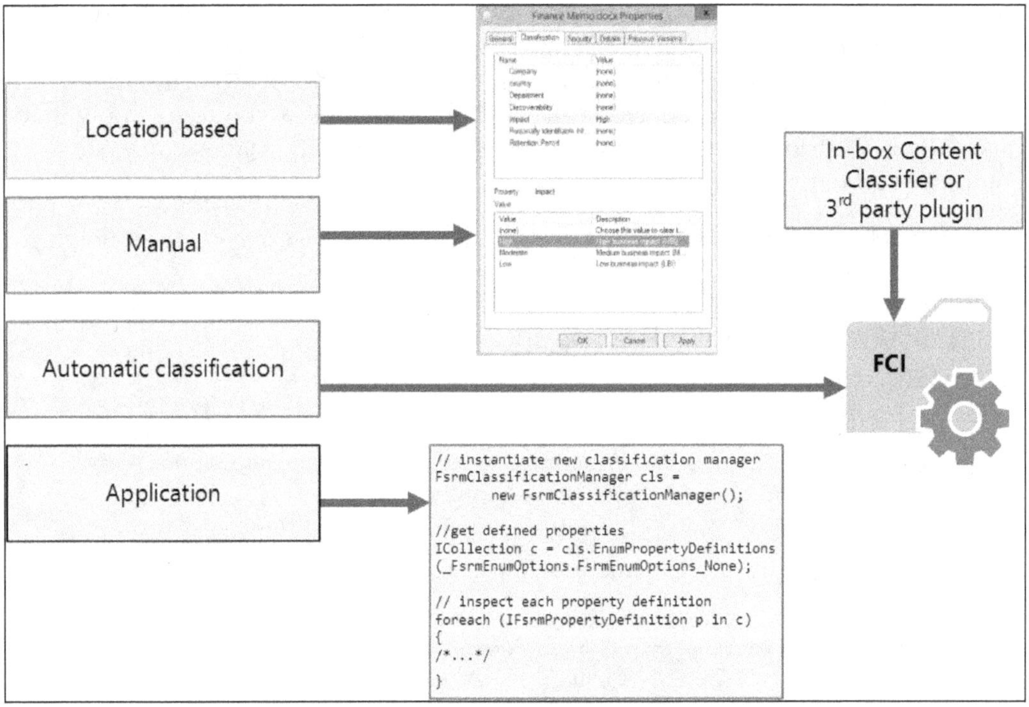

Tags identify files that are in need of protection, and they can be used to group files logically, as shown in the preceding figure. The tags are explained as follows:

- **Location-based:**
    - The folder based within the folder in which the file is created (inheritance)
    - Business owner creates the folder
- **Manual:**
    - The **Information Worker** (IW) or Administrators tag the files
    - Templates of documents (default settings)
    - Data entry applications

- **Automatic classification:**
    - Based on the content or other characteristics
    - Classifying large amounts of existing information
- **Application:**
    - **Line of Business** (**LOB**) applications that store information on file servers
    - Data management applications

Regardless of the classification method adopted, as a first step, we need to define a resource property for classifying a file as LBI, MBI, or HBI.

Let us say we want to classify a document `Finance Memo.docx`, because the information is confidential and marked by an **inovit Confidential** string in the document. So, HBI will apply for the classification. For this case, we use the **Impact** resource property that already exists. We just need to enable it in the **Active Directory Administrative Center** page:

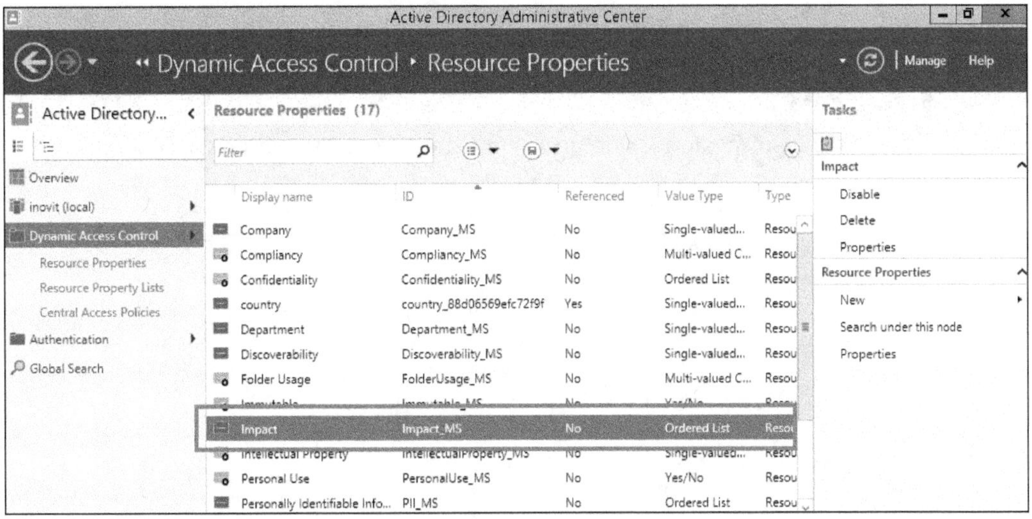

With the following equivalent PowerShell command, you can enable the resource property on the domain controller:

```
Set-ADResourceProperty -Enabled:$true -Identity:"CN=Impact_MS,CN=Resource
Properties,CN=Claims Configuration,CN=Services,CN=Configuration,DC=inovit
,DC=ch"
```

Next, we can force the synchronization of the property definitions from the domain controller to the file server. Log in to the file server and enter the following PowerShell command:

```
Update-FsrmClassificationPropertyDefinition
```

Basically, there are two methods to classify information. This was described earlier in the figure about tagging information. They are given as follows:

- Manual Classification
- Automatic Classification

Manual Classification

To manually classify a file in general, use the following tasks:

1. Open your **Windows Explorer** window and browse to the folder that contains the file you want to classify.
2. Right-click on the file name and then click on **Properties**.
3. Click on the **Classification** tab.
4. From the list of resource properties, click on the resource property you want to configure.
5. Click on the suggested value you want the resource property to use.
6. Click on **OK**.

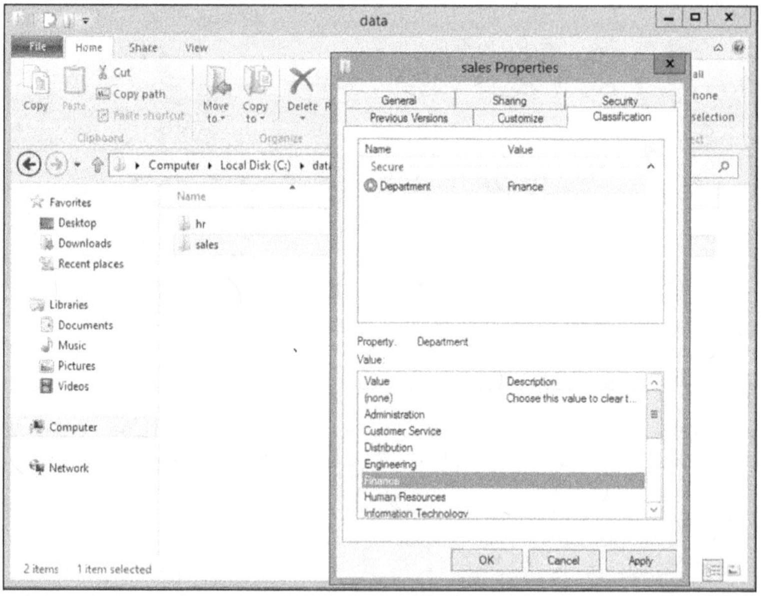

In the next few steps, we will configure the `Finance Memo.docx` example in our test lab:

1. Create a file named `Finance Memo.docx` with some sample text and the **inovit Confidential** mark.
2. Right-click on the `Finance Memo.docx` file and view the **Classification** tab to see the resource properties available for classification.

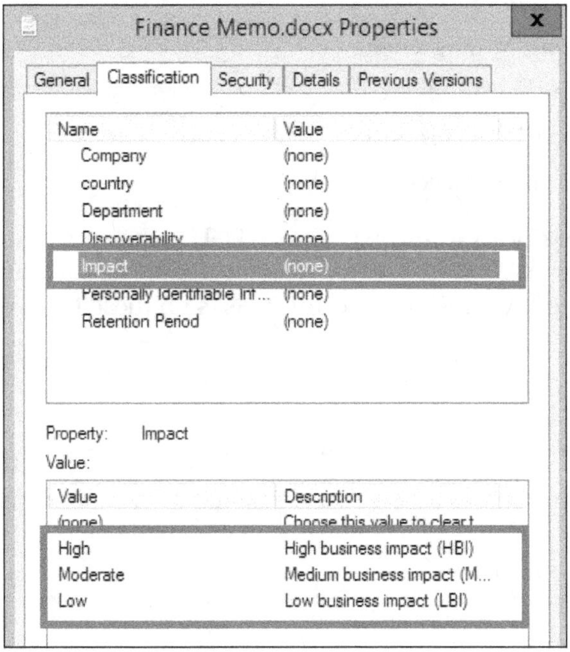

The manual classification is done by simply clicking on the **Impact** classification to set **HBI** as the defined one. This procedure can be used to classify a small amount of files. The better way is to think about the automatic classification method, which is used for a large number of files. We will discuss this in the next section.

Using the Windows File Classification Infrastructure

Since Windows 2008 R2, the **File Server Resource Manager** has built a set of features to manage and classify the data on the file servers. The main feature areas that are included in it are given as follows:

- **Quota Management**
- **File Screening Management**
- **Storage Reports Management**
- **Classification Management**
- **File Management Tasks**

For us, the **File Classification Infrastructure** (**FCI**) is the most important part of the DAC integration. With this feature, you can create rules to automatically assign specific properties to files, and then perform tasks on these files based on the classification.

For installing FSRM, use the following command:

```
Install-WindowsFeature FS-Resource-Manager
```

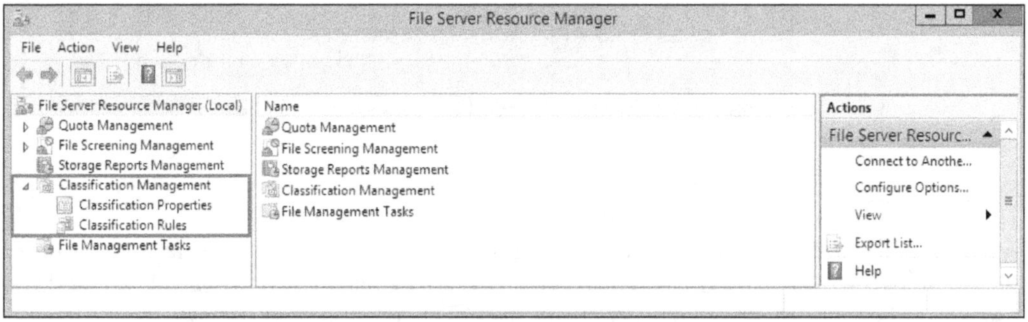

> You should install the **Microsoft Office Filter Packs** on the Windows Server 2012 and higher to enable **IFilters** for a wider array of Office files than are provided by default. Windows Server 2012 does not have any IFilters for the Microsoft Office files that are installed by default, and the FCI uses IFilters to perform content analysis. Additionally, many IFilters are available; for example, Foxit for PDF Files that is available at `http://www.foxitsoftware.com/support/showfaq_ifilter.php`.

One of the major changes to Windows 2008 R2 is that the classification properties are in the following `Active Directory` container:

```
Services - Claims Configuration - Resource Properties
```

The container is replicated to every domain controller in your environment, and you do not need to worry about configuring the same classification property on every server in your environment. You configure the properties over on the **Active Directory Administrative Center** page in the **Dynamic Access Control** section.

If you classify information automatically with FCI, the classification data is stored in an NTFS **Alternate Data Stream** (**ADS**), and the classification is maintained if you move data between different NTFS volumes. In the following screenshot, you can see our `Finance Memo.docx` example:

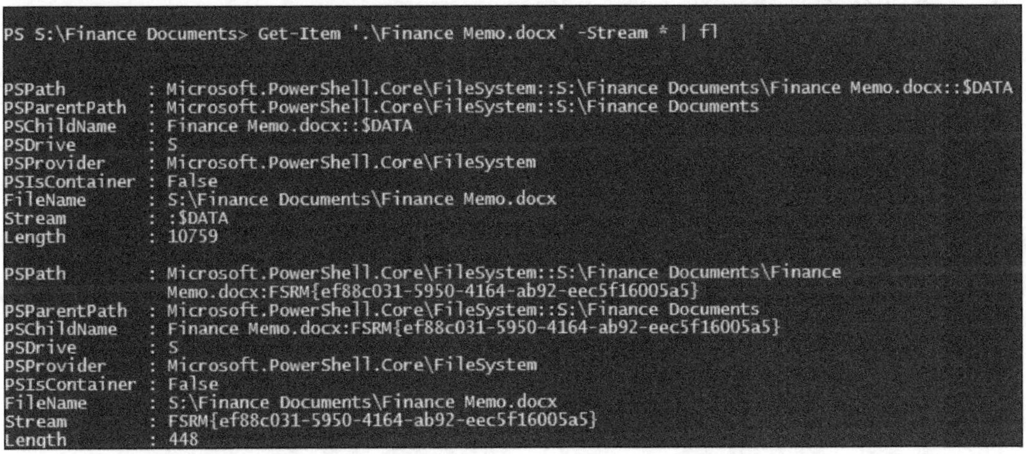

PS S:\Finance Documents> Get-Item '.\Finance Memo.docx' -Stream * | fl
PSPath : Microsoft.PowerShell.Core\FileSystem::S:\Finance Documents\Finance Memo.docx::$DATA
PSParentPath : Microsoft.PowerShell.Core\FileSystem::S:\Finance Documents
PSChildName : Finance Memo.docx::$DATA
PSDrive : S
PSProvider : Microsoft.PowerShell.Core\FileSystem
PSIsContainer : False
FileName : S:\Finance Documents\Finance Memo.docx
Stream : :$DATA
Length : 10759
PSPath : Microsoft.PowerShell.Core\FileSystem::S:\Finance Documents\Finance Memo.docx:FSRM{ef88c031-5950-4164-ab92-eec5f16005a5}
PSParentPath : Microsoft.PowerShell.Core\FileSystem::S:\Finance Documents
PSChildName : Finance Memo.docx:FSRM{ef88c031-5950-4164-ab92-eec5f16005a5}
PSDrive : S
PSProvider : Microsoft.PowerShell.Core\FileSystem
PSIsContainer : False
FileName : S:\Finance Documents\Finance Memo.docx
Stream : FSRM{ef88c031-5950-4164-ab92-eec5f16005a5}
Length : 448

Microsoft added and updated features in the File Server Resource Manager for Windows Server 2012. They are as follows:

- Dynamic Access Control (New)
- Manual (New)/Automatic Classification (Updated)
- File Management Tasks (Updated) – AD RMS integration
- Access-denied assistance (New)

In particular, we need to show the improvements in the FCI as they are very important for us. Automatic Classification has been enhanced in the following ways:

- **Continuous classification**: Classifies the data created/modified at near real-time

> You can configure continuous file classification by using the File Server Resource Manager.

- **Windows PowerShell classifier**: Enables easy implementation of custom classification logic
- **Enhanced content classifier**: Specifies the minimum and maximum occurrences of a string or regular expression
- **Dynamic name space for classification rules**: Specifies the type of information that a folder contains

In addition to the preceding additional features, the following changes are done in Windows Server 2012 R2:

- **Clear classification property values that no longer apply to an updated file**: This change enables File Server Resource Manager to dynamically remove classification values that no longer apply to a file
- **Set maximum values for storage reports:** You can configure the maximum number of files per storage report and the maximum values in the default parameters for specific storage reports.

> You can find more information on the following website: `http://technet.microsoft.com/en-us/library/dn383587.aspx`

Another important change that is interesting for developers is shown here: the `Get/Set` classification properties' APIs that are now available to non-admin accounts. Let's look at a PowerShell example so that you get an idea about what we just discussed:

```
# Get an instance of the Classification Manager
$classm = New-Object -ComObject Fsrm.FsrmClassificationManager
# Enumerate and display all properties associated with a file
$propers = $classm.EnumFileProperties("S:\CH\Zurich\Finance\Memo.docx",
0)
foreach ($prop in $propers) {
```

```
    Write-Host $prop.Name = $prop.Value
}
# Get and display the value of the "Secrecy" property
$secrecyProp = $classm.GetFileProperty("S:\CH\Zurich\Finance\Memo.docx",
"Secrecy", 0)
Write-Host $secrecyProp.Value
# Set the value of the "Secrecy" property to "High"
$classm.SetFileProperty("S:\CH\Zurich\Finance\Memo.docx", "Secrecy",
"High")
```

In the following figure, you will see the classification pipeline of the FCI, where each module passes streams of property bags to the next one. Streams can also cross processes with passing security checks. Furthermore, most of the modules are hosted within a separate process.

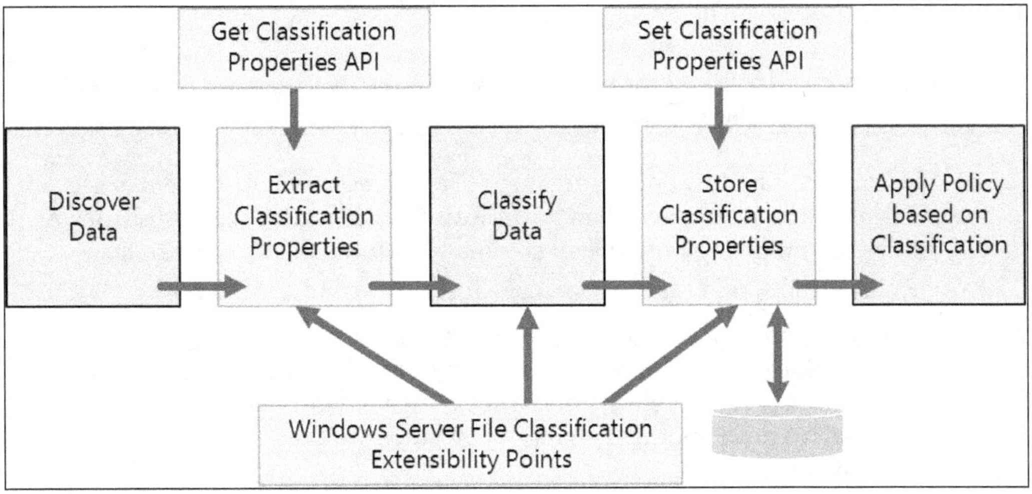

Next, we will use our `Finance Memo.docx` demo file again to configure and test the automatic classification with the FCI of our file server.

Remember that we have the **inovit Confidential** mark, which we can use to configure an automatic task that does the job for us:

1. On the file server, open **File Server Resource Manager**.
2. Under **Classification Management**, select the **Classification Rules** section.
3. Under the **Actions** pane, click on **Create Classification Rule** and create a new classification rule named `High Business Impact`.

4. Under the tabs displayed in the following table, enter the provided configuration values:

Tab	Configuration
General	**Rule name:** `High Business Impact`
Scope	• **Data: Group Files** • **Folder:** `Drive:\Finance`
Classification	• **Method: Content Classifier** • **Property: Impact** • **Value: High** Click on **Configure** under **Parameters**. Under the **Classification Parameters** dialog box, make the following selections: • **Expression Type: String** • **Expression:** `inovit Confidential` • **Occurrence:** `1`
Evaluation type	Click on **Re-evaluate existing property values** and on **Overwrite the existing value**

5. To force the classification, navigate to **Classification Management**, select **Classification Rules**, and then select **Run Classification With All Rules Now** or use the following PowerShell command to force the classification:

```
Start-FSRMClassification -RunDuration 0 -Confirm:$false
```

Another example is to use regular expressions to classify information. One typical example could be a document with **Personally Identifiable Information** (**PII**) content such as a social security number. To show you that example, we need another `Request for approval to hire.docx` file with the following content:

Information	Value
Applicant Name	`Jhonny Miller`
Social Security Number	`777-77-7777`
Job Title	`Senior Consultant`
Proposed Salary	`120'000 CHF`
Starting Date	`01.09.2013`
Supervisor Signature	`Jochen Nickel`
Approved Salary	`120'000 CHF`

Note that you can use the file for more scenarios to play around with the file and folder classification. Now, let's classify the preceding example.

6. Enable the **Personally Identifiable Information** resource property by running the following command on the domain controller:

```
Set-ADResourceProperty -Enabled:$true -Identity:"CN=PII_
MS,CN=Resource Properties,CN=Claims Configuration,CN=Services,CN=C
onfiguration,DC=inovit,DC=ch"
```

7. On the file server, run the following command:

```
Update-FsrmClassificationPropertyDefinition
```

8. To create a classification rule that sets to the **Personally Identifiable Information** property for files containing a social security number to "High", run the following command on the file server:

```
New-FSRMClassificationRule -Name "Personally Identifiable
Information Rule" -Property "PII_MS" -PropertyValue "5000"
-Namespace @("S:\Finance") -ClassificationMechanism "Content
Classifier" -Parameters @("RegularExpressionEx=Min=1;Expr=(?!000)
([0-7]\d{2}|7([0-7]\d|7[012]))([ -]?)(?!00)\d\d\3(?!0000)\d{4}$")
-ReevaluateProperty Overwrite
```

9. On the file server, run the following command:

```
Start-FSRMClassification -RunDuration 0 -Confirm:$false
```

10. Verify the file for the PII classification.

Data Classification Toolkit 2012

The **Data Classification Toolkit** is designed to help you, as an administrator, to plan and configure the classification in your file server environment. The toolkit contains sample search rules, properties, and tasks to locate, tag, and protect the data using the FCI. The standards used by the toolkit are based on the following documents:

- **Payment Card Industry Data Security Standard** (**PCI-DSS**): It is a credit card industry standard that focuses on managing protected cardholder information.
- **National Institute of Standards and Technology** (**NIST**) publications: This is a set of United States standards used to meet regulations that are applicable to federal agency IT services. This set of documents includes the following United States standards:
    - **NIST SP 800-53A**: *Guide for Assessing the Security Controls in Federal Information Systems*
    - **NIST SP 800-60 Vol1**: *Volume I: Guide for Mapping Types of Information and Information Systems to Security Categories*
    - **NIST SP 800-60 Vol2**: *Volume II: Appendices to Guide for Mapping Types of Information and Information Systems to Security Categories*

  - **NIST SP 800-122**: *Guide to Protecting the Confidentiality of PII*
  - **Federal Information Processing Standards (FIPS) Pub 199**: *Standards for Security Categorization of Federal Information and Information Systems*

The Data Classification Toolkit contains three baseline classification templates:

- **Data Classification Toolkit Package.xml**: A standard set of rules and tasks primarily focused on finding PII in data
- **NIST SP 800-53 Classification Package Example.xml**: NIST SP 800-53
- **PCI-DSS Classification Package Example.xml**: PCI-DSS

The toolkit helps you to build up a staging server, and deploy the designed and tested classification to your productive environment. For these tasks, the tools have two main applications that you can use:

- The Data Classification Toolkit wizard
- The Data Classification Toolkit Claims wizard

The Data Classification Toolkit wizard

With the Data Classification Toolkit wizard, you can walk through the process of configuring classifications:

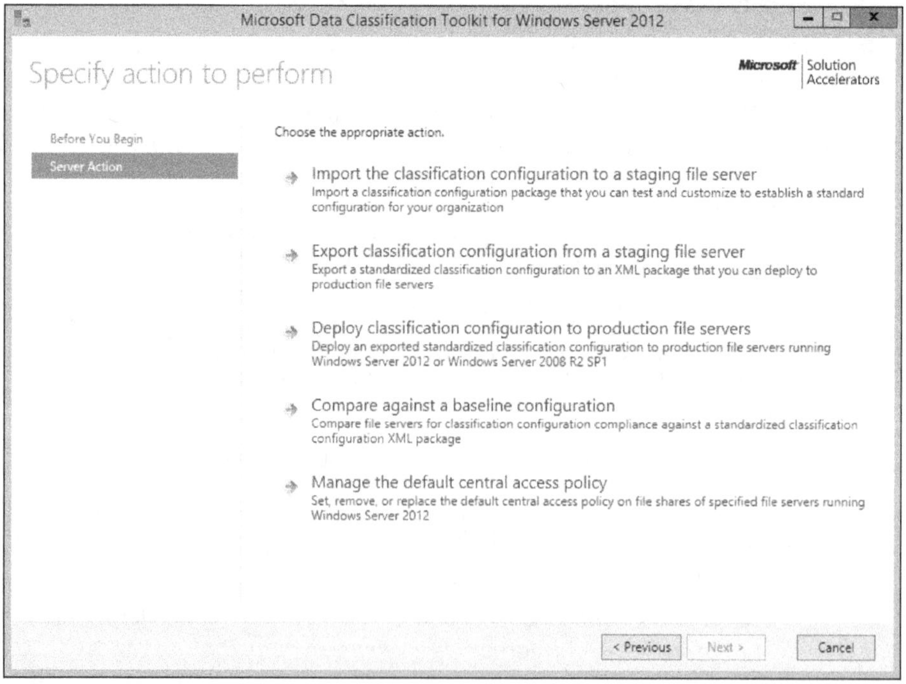

> You don't have to use the Data Classification Toolkit to import and export a classification configuration, but its templates provide a great starting point for your own rules and tasks. Alternatively, you can use PowerShell.

The following figure shows the environment and the process to work with the Data Classification Toolkit.

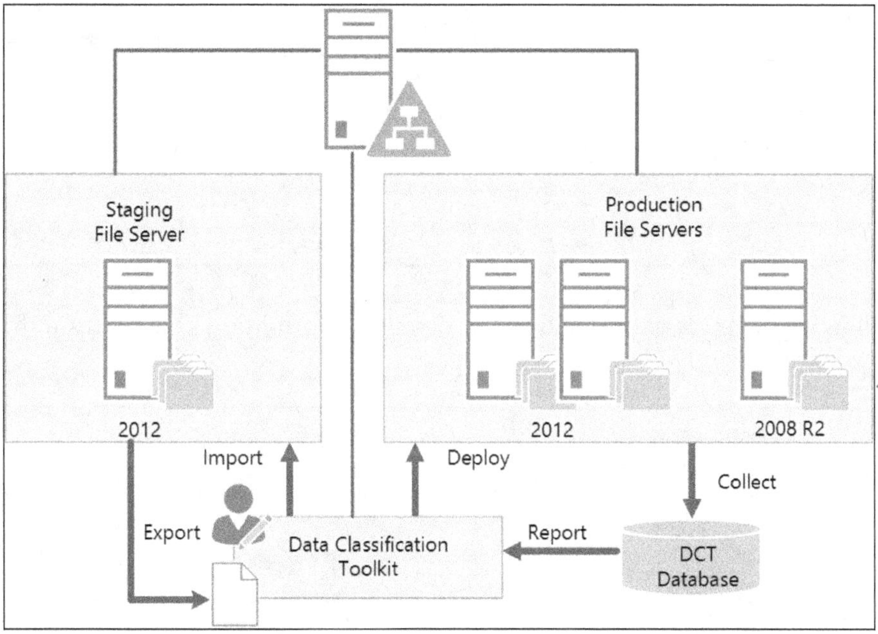

1. First, you import the baseline with the following classifications (Folder, RegEx, and PowerShell) to a staging server.
2. Next, you manage the FCI with the toolkit on a single server that configures rules and tasks.
3. Then, export your configuration and deploy the settings to all file servers in your environment.
4. Next, you collect the results to your DCT database and control the whole environment.

The Data Classification Toolkit Claims wizard

The claims wizard helps you to analyze your existing claims configuration in `Active Directory`, and is able to provide you with an Excel workbook with all the necessary information you need. In addition, you can upload your claim values to your `Active Directory` forest from an Excel workbook. These options also give you the possibility for a complete documentation of your claims configuration.

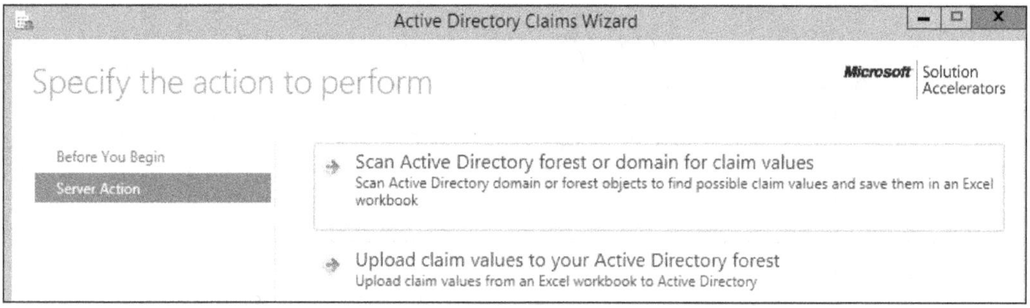

The following example export shows the detailed information you get from the claims wizard:

Claim Type	department					
Claim Type Id	ad://ext/department:88d065699dec4651					
Value	**Display Name**	**Description**	**Occurrences (User)**	**Occurrences (Computer)**	**Occurrences (Other)**	**Include**
Finance	Finance		2	0	0	No
Operations	Operations		1	0	0	No
HR	HR		2	0	0	No

Designing and configuring classifications

For trying the Data Classification Toolkit, we recommend that you refer to the *Data Classification Toolkit User Guide* at `http://www.microsoft.com/en-us/download/details.aspx?id=27123`, especially the following sections:

See the **Supported Configurations for the Data Classification Toolkit**

1. Install the Data Classification Toolkit.
2. Read and work on the **Data Classification Toolkit Scenarios**.
3. Work through the **File Classification Configuration Packages**.
4. Work through the **Viewing Data Classification Toolkit Reports**.

Summary

In this chapter, we discussed the difference between LBI, MBI, and HBI and gave you some practical examples you can directly use in your configurations. Furthermore, we defined the basic tasks to implement an automatic classification solution to help you classify information. Also, we explained the reason that the command `Update-FsrmClassificationPropertyDefinition` is a quick way to update your newly defined definitions on your file server. You also learned in which scenarios the Data Classification Toolkit can assist you. In the next chapter, we will go through the access process and the possibilities in a DAC scenario.

4

Access Control in Action

After the classification details we will discuss about creating and deploying **Central Access Policies**. We will take a closer look at FCI-integration and the Staging process (Proposed Permissions). Based on that knowledge, you will learn to identify how to access your data effectively and what happens if a user doesn't get the right permissions.

This chapter will provide you with the following topics:

- Defining the expression-based Access policies
- Deploying Central Access Policies
- Identifying Group Policy and registry settings
- Configuring FCI and Central Access Policies
- Building a staging environment using proposed permissions
- Applying your Central Access Policies
- Working scenario—identifying effective access
- Learning and using Access Denied Remediation

By the end of this chapter all the necessary information about Central Access Policies and their deployment will be covered. The lab gives you the chance to play around with a working scenario, and allows you to adopt it for your own projects.

Defining expression-based Access policies

After classifying the information, we will define the access rights that the users will have to these file resources. This can be done by configuring an expression-based access on the classified files. What this means is that we will use conditional expressions (conditional permissions) to secure the access to our information. This concept is not new; Microsoft already allows these entries with Windows 7. Conditional expressions are Boolean or logical expressions, and provide either a `TRUE` or `FALSE` result. Remember, in the prereleases of Windows Server, we used groups and group nesting to give access to resources. Just to give you a smart example of the syntax, consider the following diagram:

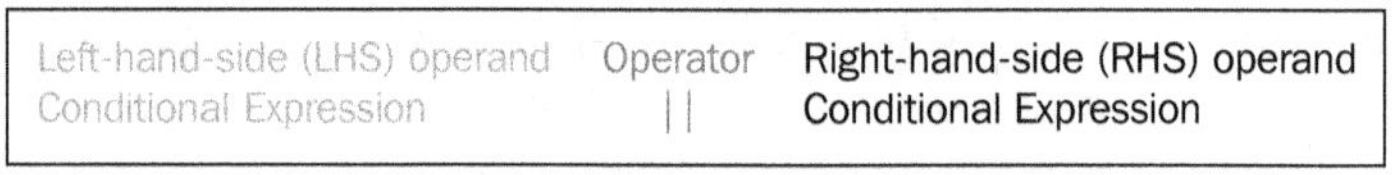

In the example, we want to give access to the file resources if the user has set the country attribute to `CH` (Switzerland) and the user department to `HR` or `Legal`:

- The **Left-hand-side (LHS) Conditional Expression** should be `@User.Country=="CH"`, which means that the user's country is "CH", that is, Switzerland
- The **Operator** should be `&&` (AND)
- The **Right-hand-side (RHS) Conditional Expression** should be `(@User.Department=="HR" || @User.Department=="Legal")`, which means that the user's department is either "HR" or "Legal")

The graphical interface to illustrate what we are doing is as follows:

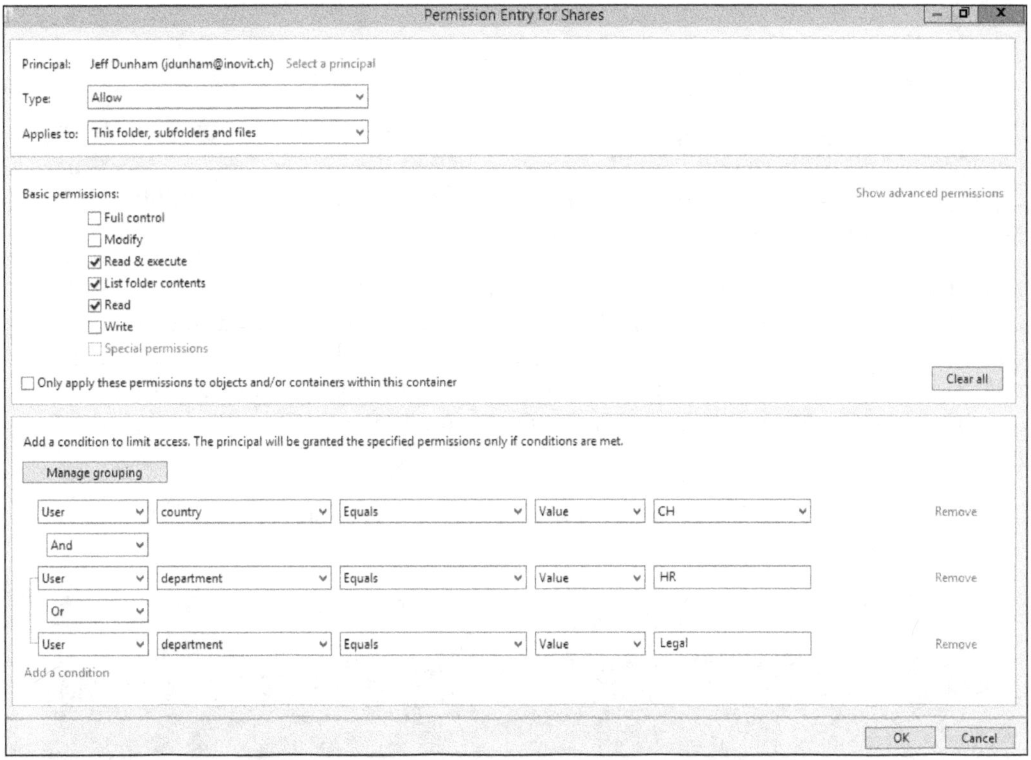

Let's evaluate the preceding interface using an example. Consider the following attributes assigned with a value:

- **User**: `Jeff Dunham`
- **Permission**: `Allow`
- **Country**: `CH`
- **Department**: `Legal`

Some important evaluation rules are as follows:

- Claims in parenthesis are evaluated first
- The == operator is evaluated before the || operator

The result for the preceding example is as follows:

```
@User.Country=="CH"
&&
(FALSE || @User.Department=="Legal")
```

The simplified format of the preceding result is `@User.Country=="CH" && TRUE`. Now, think about the second rule to proceed further. The `@User.Country=="CH"` expression will result in `TRUE`. After the `==` operator, the `&&` operator will be evaluated. This will give us the result `TRUE && TRUE`

Also, remember that in the *Manage Claims and Resource Properties* section in *Chapter 2, Understanding the Claims-based Access Model*, we discussed the `Active Directory` attributes. The conditional expression determines if the user has a claim value for `Department`. Windows does not build claims for a property without values, and if you as the administrator leave the attribute blank or fill it with a space bar, Jeff's authentication token will not include a `Department` claim.

To be sure that you set the correct attributes, you can use the `whoami /claims` command.

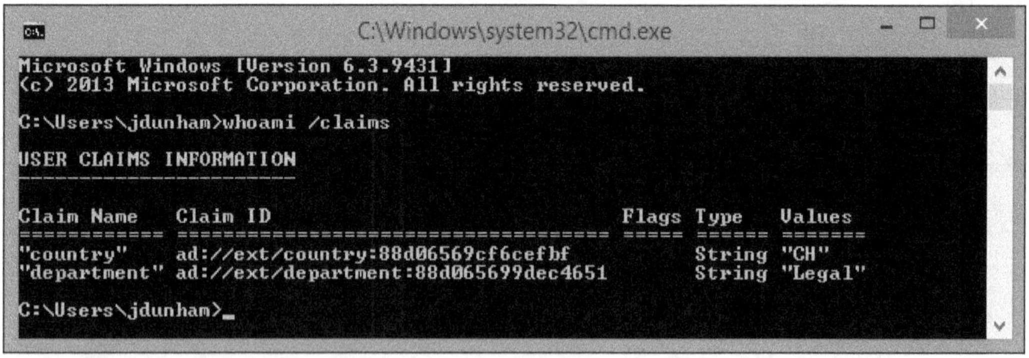

How do conditional expressions look in **Security Descriptor Definition Language (SDDL)**? Windows Server 2012 adds the conditional expressions to the **Access Control Entries** (**ACEs**) in the following format:

```
AceType;AceFlags;Rights;ObjectGuid;InheritObjectGuid;AccountSid;
  (ConditionalExpression)
```

Our example with Jeff Dunham looks as follows:

```
PS S:\Shares> Get-Acl .\Legal | fl

Path   : Microsoft.PowerShell.Core\FileSystem::S:\Shares\Legal
Owner  : BUILTIN\Administrators
Group  : INOVIT\Domain Users
Access : CREATOR OWNER Allow  FullControl
         NT AUTHORITY\Authenticated Users Allow  FullControl
         NT AUTHORITY\SYSTEM Allow  FullControl
         BUILTIN\Administrators Allow  FullControl
Audit  :
Sddl   : O:BAG:DUD:PAI(A;OICIIO;FA;;;CO)(A;OICI;FA;;;AU)(A;OICI;FA;;;SY)(A;OICI;FA;;;BA)
```

Deploying Central Access Policies

In this section, we will configure three predefined resource properties to make them available on the file server: **Confidentiality**, **Department**, and **Folder Usage**:

1. Open **Active Directory Administrative Center** (**ADAC**), navigate to **Dynamic Access Control** | **Resource Properties**, and enable the three resource properties. For example, for enabling **Folder Usage**, right-click on **Folder Usage** and click on **Enable**.
2. Right-click on **Folder usage** and click on **Properties**.
3. Under **Suggested Values**, click on **Add** and type `Finance Department Data` in the **Value** and **Display Name** fields.

Next, we create two new Central Access Rules that define the conditions to grant access to the desired scenario:

1. Open ADAC, navigate to **Central Access Rules**, and click on **New**. Type `Finance Documents Manager Rule` in the **Name** and **Description** fields.
2. In the **Target Resources** section, click on **Edit**, and in the **Central Access Rule** dialog box, click on **Add a condition**. Add the following conditions:
    - For **Department**, add the condition `Resource/Department/Equals/Value/Finance`
    - For **Confidentiality**, add the condition `Resource/Confidentiality/Equals/Value/High`
3. In the **Permission Entry for Permissions** section, add **Finance Managers** and give **Full Control**.

4. Click on the **OK** button three times to finish and return to **Active Directory Administrative Center**.
5. Now, click on **New** once more, and then type `Finance Documents Rule` in the **Name** and **Description** fields.
6. In the **Target Resources** section, click on **Edit**, and in the **Central Access Rule** dialog box, click on **Add a condition**. Add the following condition under the **Department** section:

   `[Resource]/[Department]/[Equals]/[Value]/[Finance]`
7. In the **Permission Entry for Permissions** section, add **Finance Managers** and give **Full Control**, and add **Finance Assistants** and check **Read and Execute** and **Read**.
8. In ADAC, go to **Central Access Policies** and click on **New**. Type `Finance Policy` in the **Name** field.
9. In the **Member central access rules** section, add the two new created rules.

Protecting the legal department's information with Central Access Policies

With the following example, we will demonstrate how to deploy Central Access Policies and use **File Classification Infrastructure** and **Proposed Permissions**.

First, we need to create two users for the scenario:

- `Jhonny Leano` with **Department** as `Finance`
- `Sarah Penn` with **Department** as `Finance`

Also, we need to create two global security groups for the scenario:

- `Finance Managers` with `FinanceManagers@inovit.ch` as the **E-Mail**, and add `Jhonny Leano` under the **Members** tab
- `Finance Assistants` with `FinanceAssistants@inovit.ch` as the **E-Mail**, and add `Sarah Penn` under the **Members** tab

Jhonny Leano (Finance Manager) and Sarah Penn (Finance Assistant) are colleagues in the Finance department. Jhonny should have full access to any classified file, and Sarah should only have the read rights to all of the department files, but no access to files that include credit card information and those classified as highly confidential. The files are located under `S:\CH\Zurich\Finance`.

In the example, we care about the following credit card vendors:

- **Visa**: `^4[0-9]{12}(?:[0-9]{3})?$`, all card numbers start with `4`

> New cards have 16 digits. Old cards have 13.

- **MasterCard**: `^5[1-5][0-9]{14}$`, all card numbers start with the numbers `51` through `55` and have 16 digits
- **American Express**: `^3[47][0-9]{13}$`, all card numbers start with `34` or `37` and have 15 digits

> Note that if you want to build and check your own `RegEx` library, you can use **Regex Buddy** or get a smart starter learning suite at `http://regexone.com/`.

Identifying a Group Policy and registry settings

Now that we have created our Central Access Policy including two Central Access Rules and three resource properties, we need to deploy these settings to our file server:

1. First, let us check and recap the requirements to use claims:
   - **Domain Controllers: KDC support for claims, compound authentication, and Kerberos armoring** is supported under `Computer Configuration\Policies\Administrative Templates\System\KDC`.
   - **Clients: Kerberos client support for claims, compound authentication, and Kerberos armoring** is supported under `Computer Configuration\Policies\Administrative Templates\ System\Kerberos`.

     The registry configuration location for this policy setting is located at `HKLM\Software\Microsoft\Windows\CurrentVersion\Policies\Kerberos\Parameters`.

2. Open `gpmc.msc` and expand `inovit.ch/Domains/inovit.ch`.
3. Create a GPO in this domain and link it to the **Finance Dynamic Access Control** settings:
    1. For scope/security filtering, remove **Authenticated Users** and add your file server computer account.
    2. Edit the newly created GPO and expand `Computer Configuration/Policies/Windows Settings/Security Settings/File System`.
    3. Right-click on **Central Access Policies** and then click on **Manage Central Access Policies** and add your Central Access Policy.
4. Go to your file server and fire the following commands in an administrative PowerShell console:
    - `gpupdate /force` (or you can also force the **Group Policy Update** from the GPMC on the domain controller)
    - `Update-FsrmClassificationPropertyDefinition`

Configuring FCI and Central Access Policies

Next, we will map the resource properties created in our Central Access Policy to use them in the File Classification Infrastructure. For that reason, we need to create two classification rules in the **File Server Resource Manager (FSRM)**:

- The first rule is called the **Finance Data Classification Rule**. It will classify all files under the `\\FIS01\Departments\Zurich\Finance` directory as `Finance`.
- The second rule is called the **Finance Data Sensitive Data Classification Rule**. It will automatically assign the high-confidentiality property to files that contain credit card numbers from the defined vendors.

Ok. Let's get started with creating the rules:

1. Open the FSRM on the file server:
    1. Expand **Classification Management** and open the **Classification Properties** window
    2. Then click on **Set Folder Management Properties**:
        i. Select **Folder Usage** in the **Properties** field
        ii. Add `S:\Departments\Zurich\Finance` and check **Finance Department Data**

2. In the FSRM, go to **Classification Rules** and create the classification rules defined in the preceding section:
    1. **Finance Data Classification Rule**:
        - **Scope**: Select **Finance Department Data**
        - **Classification**: Enter `Folder Classifier` under **Classification Method** and select the **Department** property and give the value as **Finance**
        - **Evaluation type**: Check **Re-evaluate existing property values** and select **Overwrite the existing value**
    2. **Finance Data Sensitive Data Classification Rule**:
        - **Scope**: Select **Finance Department Data**
        - **Classification**: Enter `Content Classifier` under **Classification Method** and select the **Confidentiality** property with the value as **High**. Then click on **Configure**. Enter three **Regular expression** entries based on the scenario description
        - **Evaluation type**: Check **Re-evaluate existing property values** and select **Overwrite the existing value**
3. Click on **Configure Classification Schedule**:
    - Check **Enable fixed schedule**
    - Check all days and check the **Allow continuous classification for new files** checkbox
4. In the Windows Explorer, navigate to the `\\FIS01\CH\Zurich\` directory and right-click on the `Finance` directory and click on **Properties**:
    1. Under the **Classification** tab, select **Department** with **Finance**.
    2. Under the **Security** tab, click on **Advanced**:
        - Disable inheritance and convert inherited permissions into explicit permissions on this object
        - Select **Authenticated Users**, click on **Edit**, allow **Full Control**, and click on **OK**
    3. Under the **Central Policy** tab, click on **Change** then select **Finance Policy**. Click twice on **OK**.

5. Test your configuration with the two users:
   1. Create a document called `Memo.docx` and add some example information.
   2. Create a document called `Credit Cards.docx` and add some example credit card numbers with the format described in the scenario.
   3. Test the access with both the users.

Building a staging environment using proposed permissions

If you want to change some conditions in a Central Access Rule, it is very important to test the new settings before you deploy them. For this reason, you can enable the staging policies to monitor the effects:

1. In the **Proposed Permissions** section of your two Central Access Rules, Finance Documents Manager Rule and Finance Documents Rule, select the **Enable permission staging configuration** checkbox and use the **Authenticated User Group** tab to add some conditions that you want to check before you deploy them.

   After configuring these settings in the Central Access Rules, navigate to your file server and fire a `gpupdate /force` command to be sure that your settings are applied.

2. Try to open documents on the **Finance** share using both of your users (Jhonny and Sarah), and for testing, create a user called Peter Kraft with an unfilled **Department** attribute in `Active Directory`.
3. Now, open **Event Viewer** on your file server and search for entries with **Event ID 4818** under the **Central Access Policy Staging** task category under `Windows Logs\Security`, and you will find the proper information about your defined staging policy.

> Keep trying with some other users and conditions to get familiar with this feature.

Applying Central Access Policies

The following steps tell you how to apply your created Central Access Policy:

1. Extend your Finance Documents Manager Rule so that the access to the `Credit Cards.docx` file is additionally limited to users that come from managed devices. In this case, you need to enable device claims.
2. Go through a staging process and change the conditions in your Central Access Rule as needed.
3. Apply your modified Central Access Rule and test your configuration with Jhonny Leano.

The preceding example scenario gives you a simple example on how you can use Central Access Policies to provide the proper permissions for any different scenario. Furthermore, you see that groups can be very nicely combined with the `Active Directory` attributes for extended scenarios and for other reasons like applications; they do not support Dynamic Access Control.

Access Denied Remediation

For **Access Denied Remediation** (**ADR**), also known as **Access-Denied Assistance**, we need to extend our basic lab deployment with an Exchange Server. For saving resources, we will install the mail server on top of the file server. If you are not familiar with installing Exchange 2013, you can follow the Microsoft Test Lab Guide at `http://social.technet.microsoft.com/wiki/contents/articles/15392.test-lab-guide-install-exchange-server-2013.aspx`.

Understanding the ADR process

Create a **File Server Administrator** account called `fisadmin`" and provide a mailbox with the **E-Mail** address, for example, `fisadmin@inovit.ch`.

Before we go further with ADR, we need to understand how the access checks are working if **Dynamic Access Control** is involved. The following figure illustrates the process:

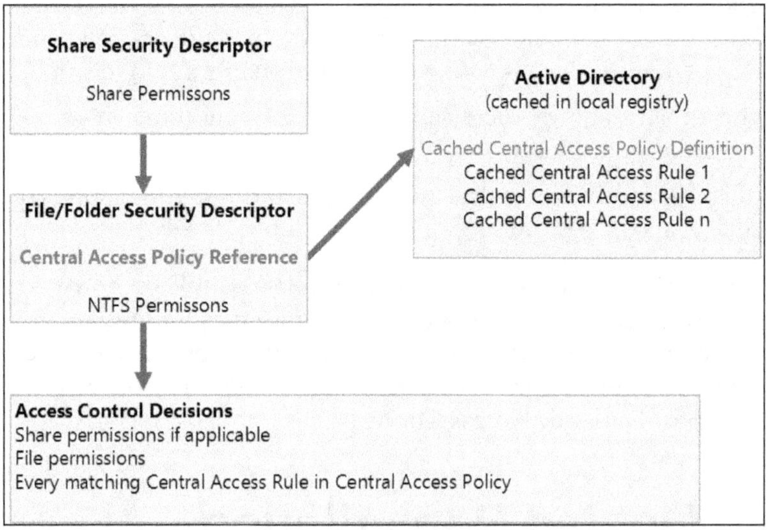

For more information about the access checks, see the following information/documents:

- `http://www.microsoft.com/en-us/download/details.aspx?id=36830`
- `http://www.frickelsoft.net/blog/?p=310`

ADR is available in two models:

- **E-Mail**: You can see the functionality by going through the Microsoft Test Lab Guide
- **Web Service Model**: We will discuss this in *Chapter 7, Extending the DAC Base Solution*

The following figure shows you the flow of ADR:

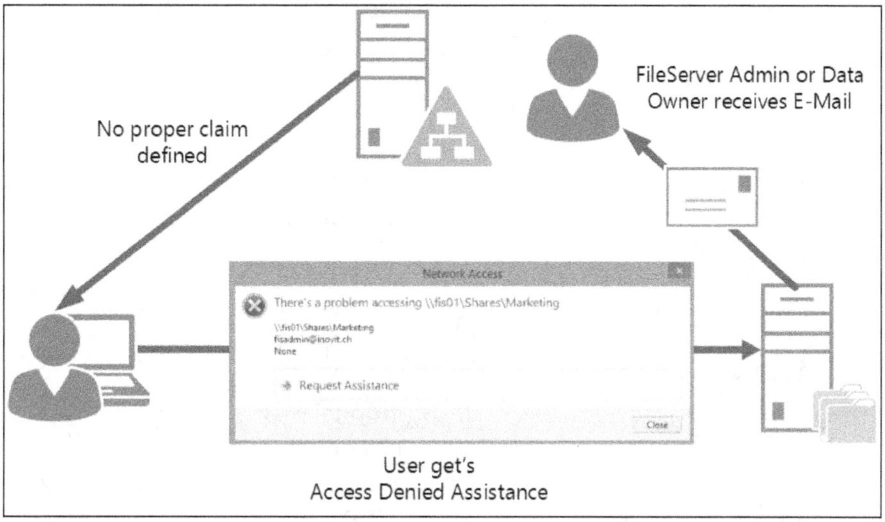

Follow the **Demonstration** steps to implement ADR to your lab. The prerequisites that are needed are configured in the e-mail settings in the FSRM, as shown in the following screenshot:

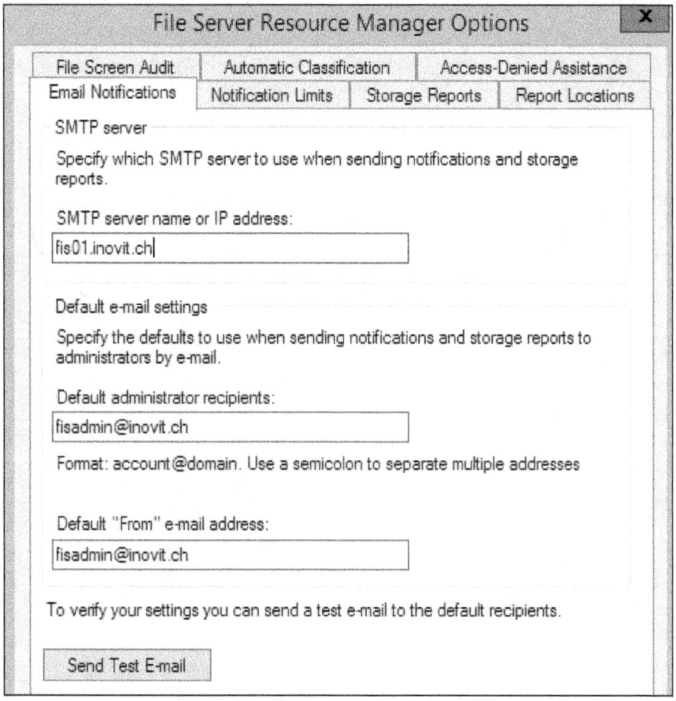

ADR – a step-by-step guide

The complete steps to implement ADR can be found under `http://technet.microsoft.com/en-us/library/hh831402.aspx`. To summarize where the settings can be managed, see the following list:

- FSRM
- Group Policy (`Computer Configuration\Policies\Administrative Templates\System\Access-Denied Assistance`)
- Powershell

Summary

In this chapter, we discussed the usage of conditional expressions and how to use them in Central Access Policies to define the correct permissions on your file servers. Please keep in touch with conditional expressions and try to make your own examples. It's always a good procedure to execute your expressions on a piece of paper, and later configure it in your lab environment. This helps you for design reasons as well as for troubleshooting. Additionally, try to build a diagram with the Share, NTFS, and Central Access Policies parts to define the correct Access-control decisions. The next chapter will provide you with the knowledge and tools to audit your Dynamic Access Control solution.

5

Auditing a DAC Solution

So far, you've learned all the necessary information about the **Central Access Policy**. Now, we will go through the auditing process of a **Dynamic Access Control** solution and will help you to address the requirements of the **Chief Information Security Officer** (**CISO**) and the data owners.

In this chapter we will discuss the following topics:

- Using conditional expressions for auditing
- Claims-based Global Object Access Auditing
- Configuring an effective auditing solution
- Policy considerations
- How System Center extends the solution

After studying this chapter, you'll be prepared to assist your colleagues in dealing with Information Security, and this will definitely make them happy.

Auditing with conditional expressions

In Windows Server 2012, you are able to define the expression-based audit policies. This functionality enables you to create audit policies based on user, computer, and resource claims. For example, if you want to be aware of all the types of read operations on confidential-classified files, you can now do this centrally over Group policies or directly and manually on the file server. Group policies give you the advantage of monitoring the following scenarios and components:

- Central Access Policies
- Resource Attribute Definitions
- Central Access Policy and Rule definitions

- Claim types and user/device claims during sign-ins
- Resource attributes on files and folders
- Central Access Policies associated with files and folders

The following screenshot shows you where you can manually configure auditing in the **Advanced Security Settings** editor on the server:

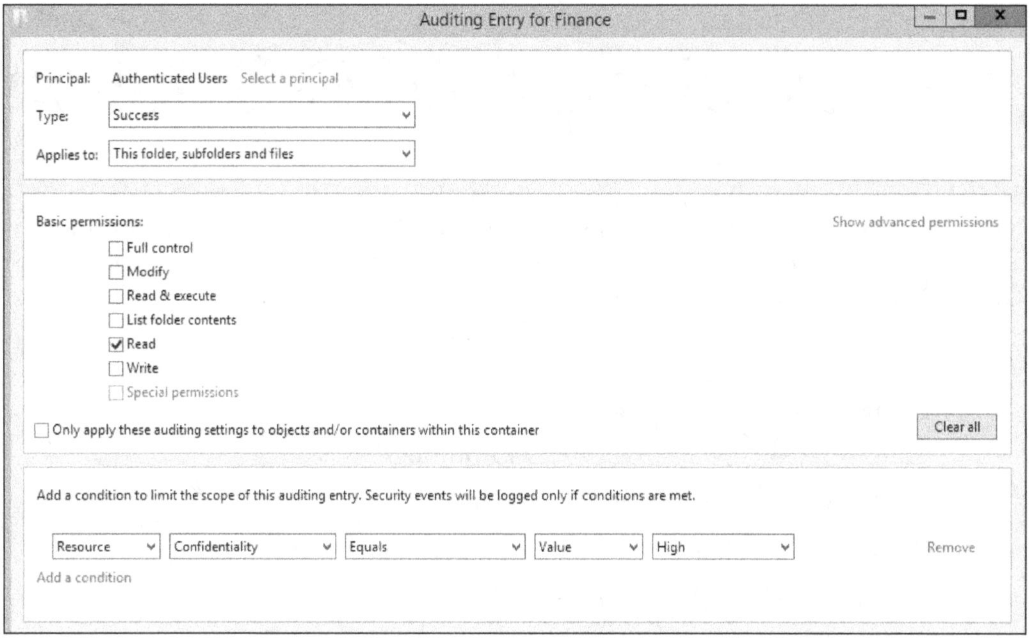

Claims-based Global Object Access Auditing

With the **Global Object Access Auditing** settings, you now have a centrally managed feature set to manage your Windows Server auditing solution. Keeping the preceding example in mind, we had to go to the file server itself to configure the expression-based auditing settings. You can do the same and much more with the **Group Policy** settings as shown in the following screenshot:

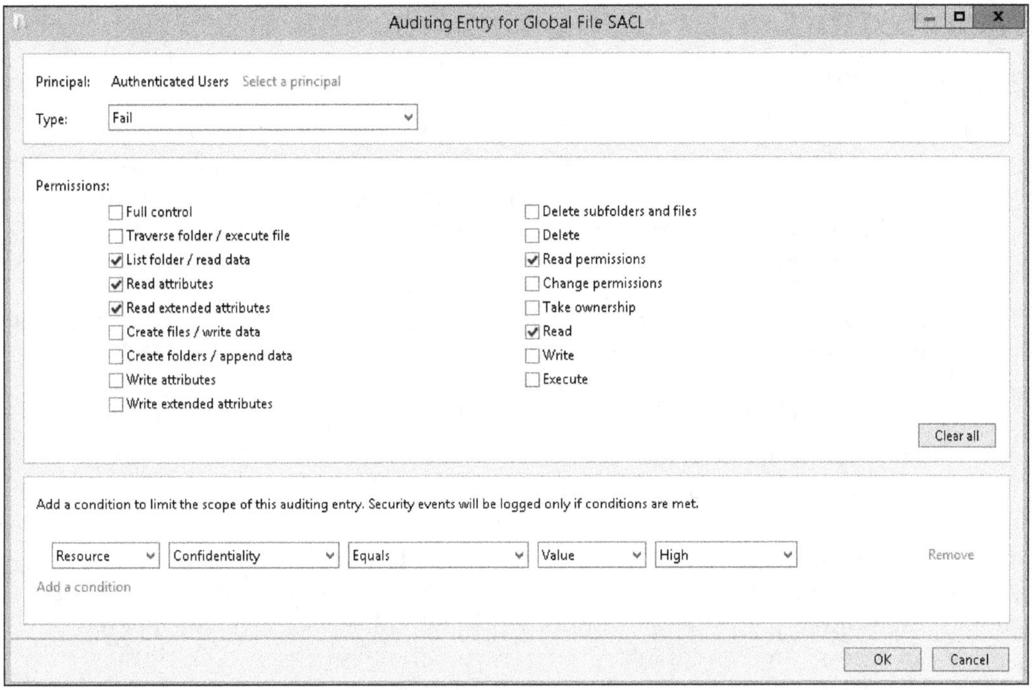

To give you a better idea of the powerful functionality available, we will show some examples in the following section. In the next screenshot, you'll see the different main sections in the Group Policy editor under `Computer Configuration\Policies\Windows Settings\Security Settings`:

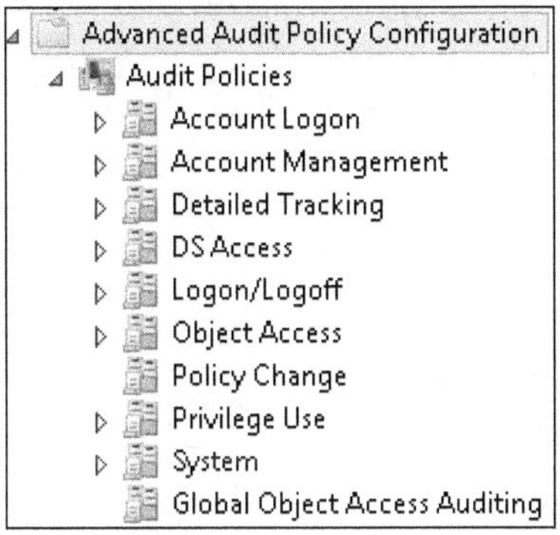

Monitoring your Dynamic Access Control scenarios

Not only is monitoring file access a necessity in your environment, but you also need to know who makes changes and at what time changes are made to the security configuration in the organization. Additionally, you need to think about your resource properties, specifically whether or not they are relevant for the file classification tasks on your file server.

The following reasons are examples of why you need to monitor resource properties on files and folders:

- Business impact changes
- Retention value changes
- Department value changes

If the associated Central Access Policies are changed in the wrong way and applied on your file server environment, the results can be a security breach. For example, people who normally have access cannot work with their files, or unauthorized people can access confidential information if you do not integrate **AD Rights Management Services** (**AD RMS**) into your DAC solution.

Enable the monitoring results in the addition of specific entries in the **Security Log** of the domain controllers/file servers. The following table gives you useful and practical information about the different monitoring scenarios:

Monitoring scenario	Main configuration	Relevant Event ID's (Security Log)	Main reason
Central Access Policies	Advanced Audit Policy Configuration	4819	Changes in the security configuration in your organization
Resource Attribute Definitions	Advanced Audit Policy Configuration Active Directory Administrative Center	5137	Relevance of file classification tasks
Central Access Policy and Rule Definitions	Advanced Audit Policy Configuration Active Directory Administrative Center	4819	Changes in the access control configuration in your organization

Monitoring scenario	Main configuration	Relevant Event ID's (Security Log)	Main reason
User and Device Claims during Sign-in	Advanced Audit Policy Configuration	4626 with information about user/device claims	Usage of claims
Resource Attributes on Files and Folders	Advanced Audit Policy Configuration	4911 file attribute changes 4913 CAP changes	Business impact changes Retention value changes Department value changes
Central Access Policies Associated with Files and Folders	Advanced Audit Policy Configuration Windows Explorer	4913 SID's of the old/new CAP	CAPs are changed on your file server environment: wrong access permissions
Claim Types	Advanced Audit Policy Configuration Active Directory Administrative Center	5137	Usage of claims

You can find the step-by-step instructions on `http://technet.microsoft.com/en-us/library/dn319102.aspx`.

Configuring an effective auditing solution

Now that we know all the options we need to configure the audits for, we can configure a starter auditing solution inside your file server environment. The solution covers the access of unauthorized persons to the finance department share and tracks it. Follow the steps to configure a global object access policy:

1. Sign in to your domain controller **ADS01** and start **gpmc.msc**.
2. Expand `inovit.ch\Domains\inovit.ch`.
3. Create a new GPO called **Finance Data Auditing Policy** and link it to the domain.
4. Set the security filtering only to your file server.
5. Double-click on **Computer Configuration**, double-click on **Policies**, double-click on **Windows Settings**, and double-click on **Security Settings**.

6. Then double-click on **Advanced Audit Policy Configuration**, double-click on **Audit Policies**, double-click on **Object Access**, and double-click on **Audit File System**.
7. Select the **Configure the following events** checkbox, select the **Success** and **Failure** audit event checkboxes, and then click on **OK**.
8. Double-click on **File system** under the **Global Object Access Auditing** section.
9. Click on the **Define this policy setting** checkbox and click on **Configure**.
10. In the **Advanced Security Settings for Global File SACL** box, click on **Add**, then on **Select a principal**, type `Everyone`, and then click on **OK**.
11. In the **Auditing Entry for Global File SACL** box, select **Full control** in the **Permissions** box.
12. In the **Add a condition** section, click on **Add a condition**, and in the drop-down list, select **[Resource] [Department] [Any of] [Value] [Finance]**.
13. Click on **OK** three times to complete the configuration of the global object access audit policy settings.
14. Click on **Object Access**, and then double-click on **Audit Handle Manipulation**.
15. Click on **Configure the following audit events**, select **Success** and **Failure** under that, click on **OK**, and then close the GPO.

> Additionally, configure all the previously described policy settings and play around with the solution. Install the JiJi Audit Reporter to integrate a third-party tool at `http://www.jijitechnologies.com/dynamic-access-control-effective-permission-report.aspx`.

Policy considerations

Obviously, the monitoring resources in an organization are limited, but you need to have a well-defined strategy to track the access and configuration of the organizations' most important resources. Regulatory compliance is one of the main targets of security audits. Furthermore, security audits help you to identify and minimize gaps in your security policies and detect uncommon behavior.

Think about the four main steps to configure auditing and deriving the results:

- Identify the correct set of data and users to monitor
- Create and apply appropriate audit policies
- Collect and analyze audit events
- Manage and monitor the policies that were created

Your security audit policy should include a minimum of the following items:

- Protection of the organization's data and intellectual property
- Regulatory requirements
- Users (including employees such as FTE and PTE), vendors, contractors, partners, resellers, and customers
- Client and server computers with applications and services running

Extending the solution with System Center

With the **Audit Collection Service** (**ACS**) of the System Center Operations Manager 2012, you are able to collect the security audit information generated by an audit policy in a central database. Using ACS helps you to consolidate security log information and gives you the option to analyze the information and provide proper reports to your CISO.

ACS requires the following components:

- **ACS Forwarders**: It enables audit collection; all security events are sent to the ACS Collector
- **ACS Collector**: It receives and processes events from ACS Forwarders and sends the data to the ACS Database
- **ACS Database**: The ACS Database is a central repository for events that are generated by an audit policy within an ACS deployment. You can find more details at `http://technet.microsoft.com/en-us/library/hh212908.aspx`

> You can find the installation instructions at `http://technet.microsoft.com/en-us/library/hh284670.aspx` and `http://technet.microsoft.com/en-us/library/hh299397.aspx`.

The following figure shows the principal extension for our used test environment:

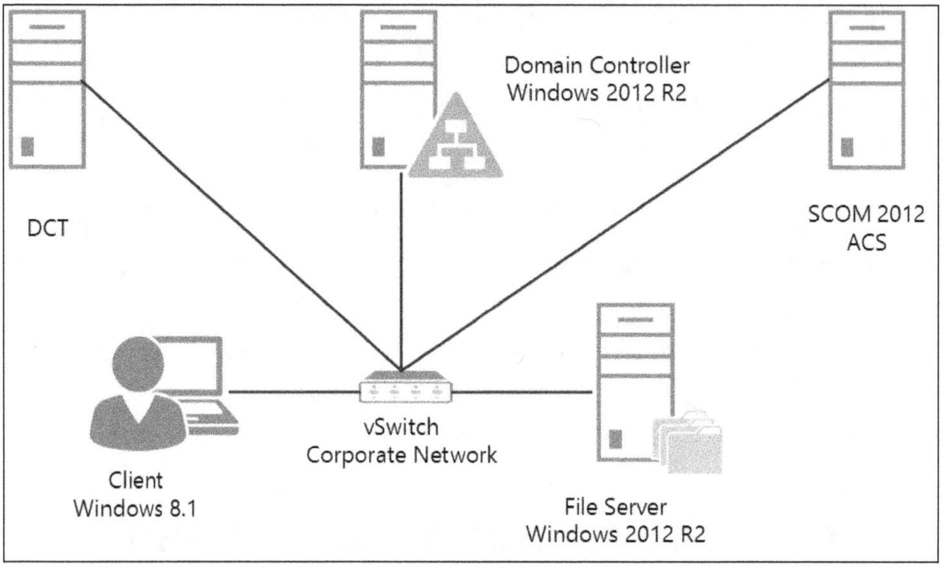

For using ACS, no extra configuration on the Dynamic Access Control side is necessary. With the reporting capabilities of SQL Server, you have an open tool set to configure your own user-defined reports.

Summary

In this chapter, we provided all the important information about using conditional expressions for auditing your Dynamic Access Control solution. In addition, we discussed all the steps you need to define and configure claims-based Global Object Access Auditing options. The System Center Suite is increasingly important and helps you to enrich the functionality for auditing your relevant configurations. Next, we will discuss the integration of AD RMS to protect your information on the file servers and any other place.

6
Integrating Rights Management Protection

In this chapter, we will discuss the integration of **Active Directory Rights Management Services** (**AD RMS**) with the DAC solution. In a practical scenario, we show the importance of AD RMS accomplish a complete information protection solution. In this chapter, we will cover the following topics:

- Windows Server 2012 Active Directory Rights Management Services
- Configuring AD RMS to work with DAC
- Function of Rights Protected Folder
- How Classification-based Encryption works
- Protecting your information using a combination

By the end of this chapter, you will be able to adopt AD RMS to your DAC solution. If your company wants to implement an information protection concept, you can start working smoothly and calmly on such a project.

Windows 2012 AD RMS

AD RMS include all the client and server components that are required to support information protection in your organization. AD RMS allows you to build an organization's security strategy to protect information through persistent usage policies that stay with the information wherever you place it. For example, you can use AD RMS to protect financial information, development results, and new product specifications from unauthorized access. Another important aspect is that you can define even the most minute permissions on an AD RMS protected file. For example, you can provide a read-only access, but printing or copying and pasting some information from the document can be disabled.

The technology is based on a set of web service components running on the **Internet Information Services (IIS)** communication with SQL Server and the Active Directory. For extending the authentication part, you can integrate the **Active Directory Federation Services (ADFS)** in an AD RMS solution. The following figure gives you an idea about the AD RMS architecture and the different components building the solution. For special considerations, you can extend the solution with many third-party vendors. You see a vendor list in the following figure under the **Third-party Extensions** part.

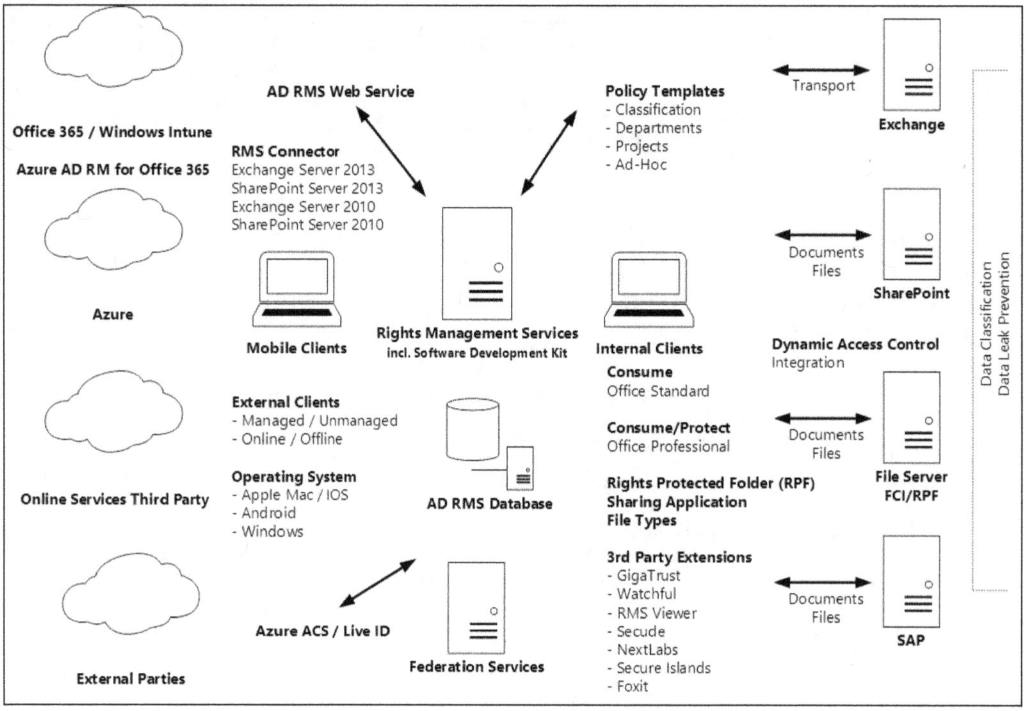

AD RMS, like any IT service, relies on some infrastructure to function. In the case of AD RMS, several components work together for the solution to deliver a useful service. The most relevant ones are:

- AD RMS servers and clusters
- AD RMS SQL Server database
- Active Directory
- AD Rights Management Services client and RMS-enabled applications in the client
- AD RMS-integrated server applications

With AD RMS, you have a broad range of permissions that you can set for your information; it's more than just encrypting some information. The following screenshot gives you an idea about the permissions:

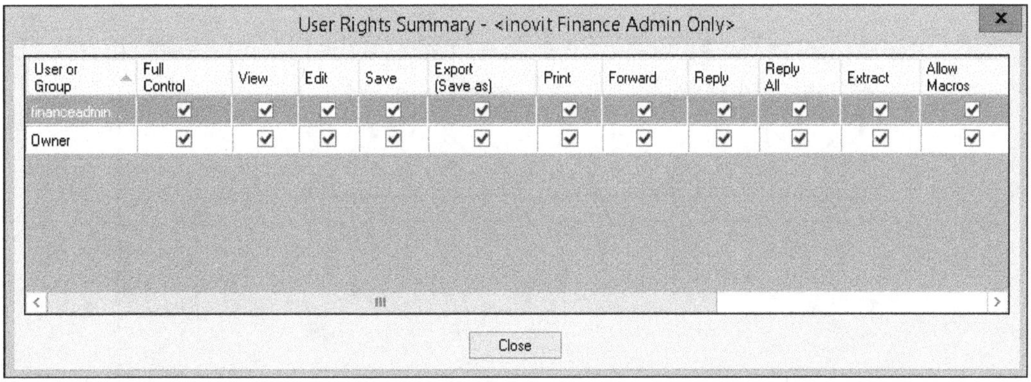

> You find more information about the permissions at `http://technet.microsoft.com/en-us/library/dd996658(v=ws.10).aspx`.

To understand the basic functionality, we use a simple example with a simplified AD RMS infrastructure. Let us say, for example, Jhonny Leano (Finance Manager) wants to protect some financial reports that only his department can use, and if the documents leave the organization, they need to be protected against any unauthorized access.

1. Jhonny applies access restrictions and the AD RMS client initiates a service request to the AD RMS server.
2. The AD RMS server returns a Client Licensor Certificate to the AD RMS client. This enables Jhonny to save the document that is encrypted with the desired level of protection.
3. Jhonny sends the encrypted document to Sarah Penn (Finance Assistant), a colleague of Jhonny's.
4. Sarah opens the encrypted document and at this moment, the AD RMS client contacts the AD RMS server to acquire an end-user license. The AD RMS client receives the end-user license that allows Sarah to read the information defined by Jhonny's access restrictions.

> It will also ask for a username and password if the AD RMS Server address is not in the Internet Explorer's local intranet site or if the computer is not part of the Active Directory.

The following figure shows the AD RMS flow based on the previous description:

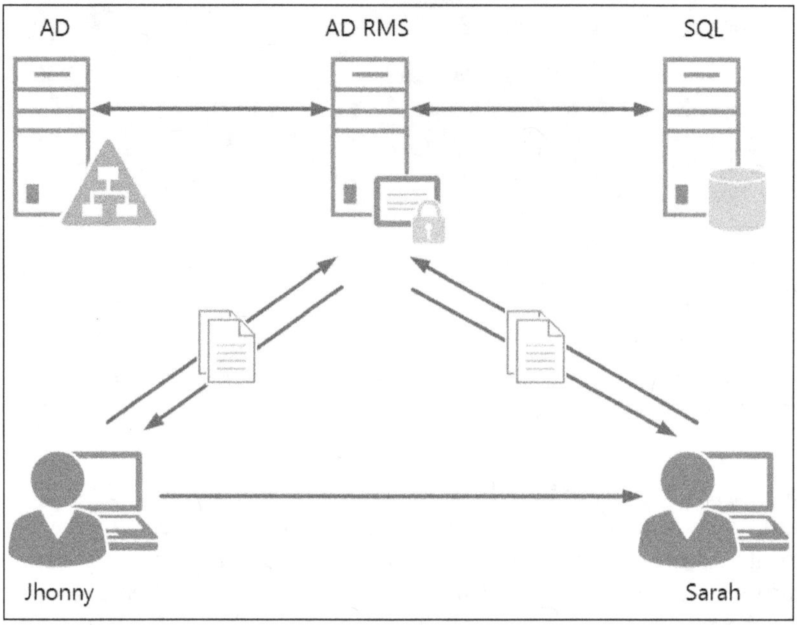

Installing Rights Management Services

First, we need to extend our test-lab environment with AD RMS. For this reason, we add the AD RMS role on the file server that is not recommended in a productive environment. However, we do not want to bring another server in the game, but feel free if you want to use the lab for testing AD RMS in a productive scenario; you can install and configure your servers for your needs. For our scenario, follow the steps in the **Install Active Directory Rights Management Services** section in the *TechNet* article at `http://technet.microsoft.com/en-us/library/hh831776.aspx`, and use your file server FIS01 for installation.

> If you want to go further with AD RMS, you can also try the following test lab guide: `http://technet.microsoft.com/en-us/library/adrms-test-lab-guide-base.aspx`

Now that we have extended our test-lab scenario, we can start using the AD RMS component to protect our sensitive information. We will go further with our finance department example. Remember Jhonny and Sarah and the classified documents containing credit card information with **Confidential=High**? To protect these documents, like we discussed in the simplified AD RMS flow, we want to protect those files with an additional layer of security. Furthermore, there are some AD RMS limitations on the file types that need our attention. Basically, AD RMS supports MS Office and XPS files with built-in functionality. If you need to protect other file formats like PDFs or JPEGs, you have some options to solve that issue. One option is to integrate third-party extensions that fill the gap, and the other option is to use the Rights Protected Folder from Microsoft. This is an additional component that you can use to protect other file formats.

Note that Microsoft provides the **Microsoft Rights Management sharing application** with the following feature set:

- Protecting any file with user-authored permissions in place
- Protecting and sharing any file using e-mail
- Allowing generic protection for any file type including MS Office and PDF files
- Allow MS Office 2010 to work with Windows Azure Active Directory Rights Management
- Adding new buttons to the MS Office toolbar for Word, PowerPoint, and Excel

> Supported file types can be found at `http://technet.microsoft.com/en-us/library/dn339003(v=ws.10).aspx#BKMK_SupportedFiles`.

Rights Protected Folder

Rights Protected Folder (**RPF**) is a Windows-based application that allows you to protect files and folders. Its quite simple; you have a folder that contains files and folders that you want to protect with AD RMS. Using RPF, you can securely protect your sensitive information or send it to somebody who will be able to access those files based on a desired AD RMS level.

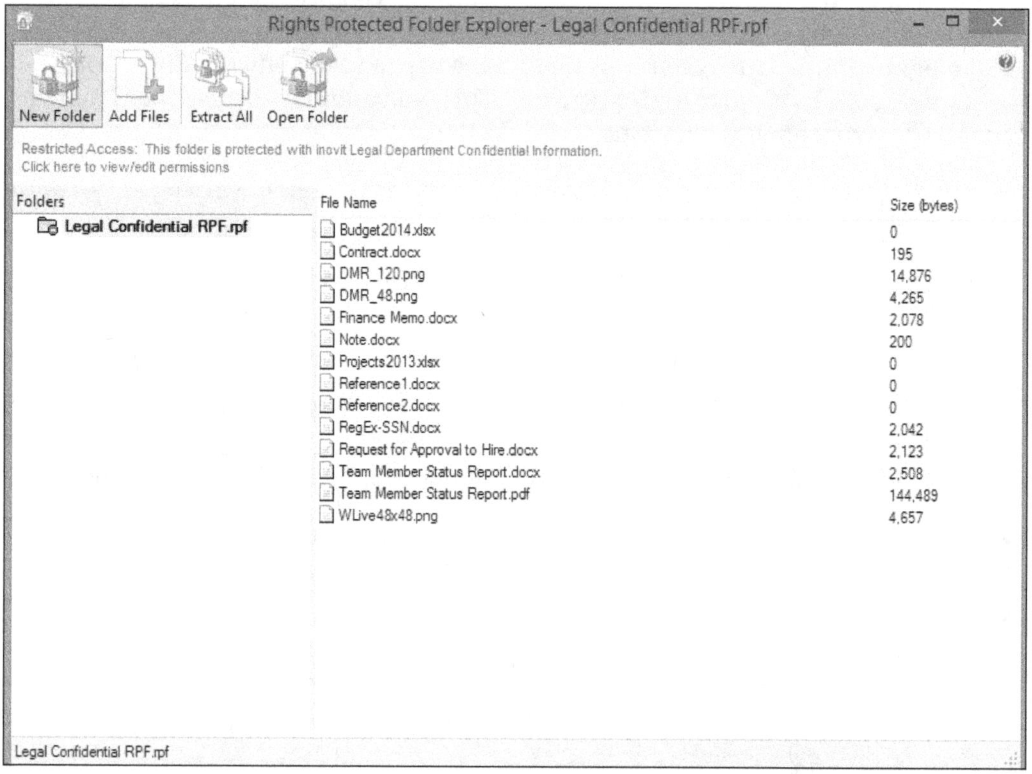

RPF is not only available on the client side, it also integrates with the File Classification Infrastructure. This gives you, as the file server administrator, the possibility to protect any file on a file server with AD RMS. Once the files are protected, only authorized users will be able to access those files even if they are copied to another location. To protect non-Microsoft Office file formats, you can use **File Management Task** (**FMT**) with custom actions to use the RPF.

To use RPF with the **File Classification Infrastructure** (**FCI**), you need to follow the steps provided at `http://blogs.technet.com/b/filecab/archive/2012/10/15/automatic-rms-protection-of-non-ms-office-files-using-fci-and-rights-protected.aspx`.

> Another option to protect PDF files, for example, is to use Foxit Enterprise Reader with the Foxit RMS plugin. See an example at `http://blogs.technet.com/b/rms/archive/2012/11/09/protect-everything-using-fci-to-protect-files-of-any-type-with-windows-server-2012.aspx`.

Classification-based encryption

With Windows Server 2012 FCI, you have the option to automatically encrypt sensitive files based on their classifications. Within a few seconds, the file is identified as sensitive information, and a continuous file management task will apply the AD RMS protection to the file based on the configured AD RMS template. The following actions apply in this scenario:

- For a file server:
    - An administrator configures automatic classification
    - A data owner configures location-based classification
- For a client:
    - A user saves a document containing sensitive information on the file server
- For FCI:
    - Automatic classification detects sensitive information and encrypts the document

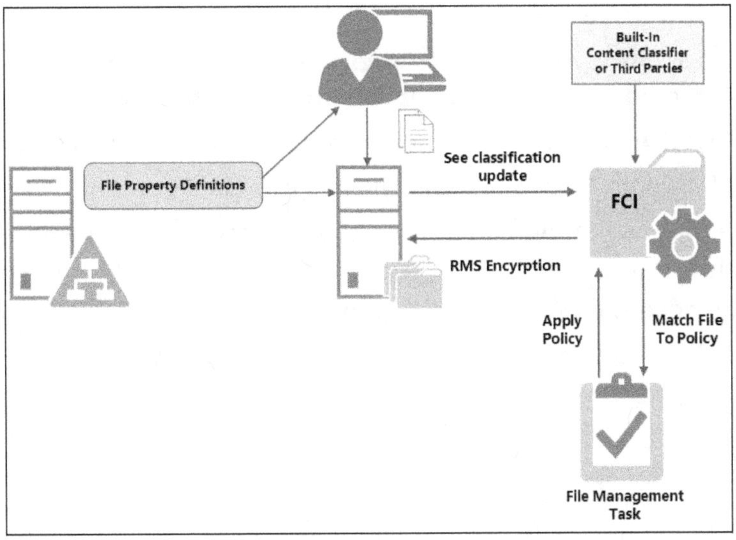

Protecting your information with a combination

To get more familiar with Classification-based encryption, we go through the following steps for extending our finance example, as discussed in the previous section. The main tasks are:

1. Create the rights-management template for confidential information in the Finance department.
2. Create an encryption rule using a File Management Task.
3. Test the access to the classified and encrypted documents.
4. Building the RPF example in your environment.
5. Use file retention for our example.

The rights management template

A rights management template can be created as follows:

1. Log in to FIS01 as `inovit\administrator`.
2. Navigate to **Start** | **Administrative Tools** | **Active Directory Rights Management Services**.
3. Expand the cluster `fis01.inovit.ch` under **Rights Policy Templates**.
4. In the **Actions** pane, click on **Create Distributed Rights Policy Template** to start the wizard.
5. In the wizard, click on **Add**.
6. In the **Language** list, select **US language** and type `Finance Department Confidential Information` in both the **Name** and **Description** boxes.
7. Click on **Add** and type `FinanceManagers@inovit.ch` as the e-mail address.
8. Give full control rights to `FinanceManagers@inovit.ch`.
9. In **Specify Expiration Policy**, check **Use license expiration** and set it to one day.
10. In **Extended Policy**, check the first two checkboxes.

Encryption rule

An encryption rule can be created as follows:

1. Log in to FIS01 as `inovit\administrator`.
2. Navigate to **Start** | **Administrative Tools** | **File Server Resource Manager**.
3. Create a File Management Task.
4. In the **General** tab, type `Encryption of Finance Department Confidential Information`.
5. In the **Scope** tab, check **Finance Department Data**.
6. In the **Actions** tab, select **RMS Encryption** and the **Finance Department Confidential Information** template.
7. In the **Condition** tab, click on **Add**.
8. Now select **Confidentiality** as **Property**, **Equal** as **Operator**, and **High** as **Value**.
9. In the **Schedule** tab, check all the days and Run continuously on new file.

Information access

You can test information access as follows:

1. Connect as Sarah Penn to the Finance share.
2. Connect as Jhonny Leano to the Finance share.
3. Create a new file called `Credit Card Update.docx` with some example credit card numbers.
4. Create a new file called `Credit Card Renewal.docx` with some example credit card numbers, and save it.
5. See the results for the old and the new files.

Building the RPF example in your environment

Try integrating the Rights Protected Folder to your environment with the previous description, and play around with this feature set to see the different behaviors on the finance file share.

File retention

Next, we will extend our solution so that the encrypted files are automatically moved to a special directory called `Confidential` under `S:\CH\Zurich\Finance` every day.

1. In the **File Server Resource Manager** (**FSRM**) console, create a new File Management Task.
2. Under the **General** tab, enter the task name as `Move Finance Confidential and Encrypted files`.
3. Under the **Scope** tab, select the Finance department data and folder located at `S:\CH\Zurich\Finance`.
4. In the **Type** box under the **Action** tab, select **File expiration**.
5. Choose the Expiration directory as `S:\CH\Zurich\Finance\Confidential`.
6. Under the **Notification** tab, click on **Add**, and select the **Send an e-mail to users with affected files** checkbox.
7. Define the subject as `Finance Confidential Files are moved to S:\CH\Zurich\Finance\Confidential`.
8. Under the **Condition** tab, add the following properties:
    - Select **Confidential** in the **Property** list
    - Select **Equal** in the **Operator** list
    - Select **High** in **theValue** list
9. In the **Schedule** tab, click on the **Weekly** option and check all the days. Select the **Run at** time as 11 pm.
10. Test your configuration by changing the **Run at** time of the task.

> Microsoft provides new functionalities in AD RMS. For more information, go to the following link:
>
> `http://blogs.technet.com/b/rms/archive/2013/08/29/the-new-microsoft-rms-is-live-in-preview.aspx`

If you want to use your AD RMS templates for personal use in the Office suite, you can deploy the templates to your client computer using this procedure.

For this reason, you can use scripts or the pre-defined schedule task in Vista SP1 and higher versions. The task is disabled by default, and can be activated with the following command:

```
schtasks /Change /TN "\Microsoft\Windows\Active Directory
  Rights Management Services Client\AD RMS Rights Policy
  Template Management (Automated)" /ENABLE
```

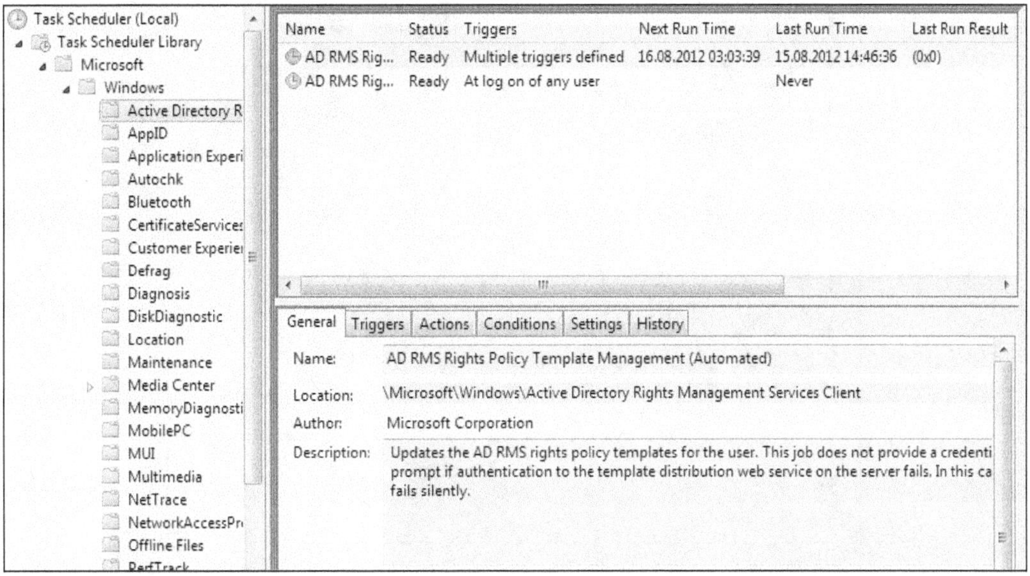

If the task is enabled, the only thing that needs to be done is to configure the template's download path. The path can be configured by group policies with templates for your MS Office version or with the following key:

```
HKEY_CURRENT_USER\Software\Microsoft\Office\14.0\Common\DRM
```

AD RMS in a SAP environment

Another interesting fact is that you can use AD RMS not only in your file server environment but also for a SAP environment. There is a solution in the market to secure documents downloaded from a SAP NetWeaver environment. The following figure shows the architecture of the solution:

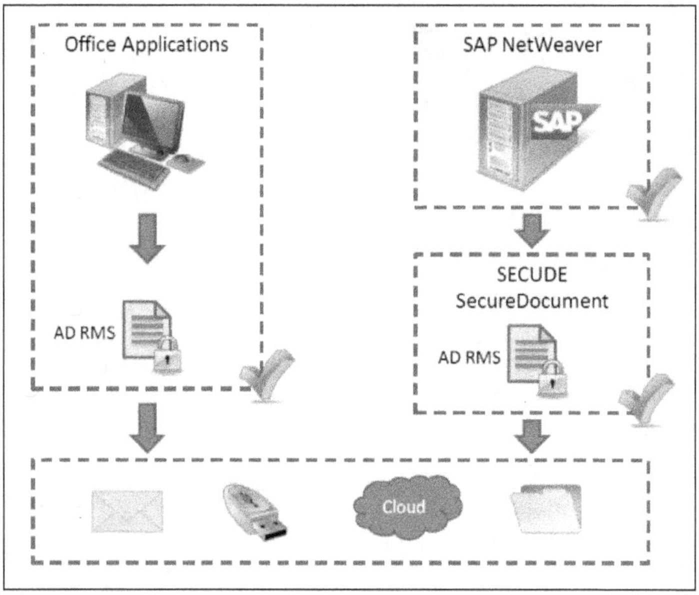

The solution is Halocore from the data security provider, SECUDE. Halocore intercepts data downloads from SAP Business Suite or Business Warehouse to MS Office Applications, file servers, or an end user's computer by introducing an AD RMS access envelope that envelops the data, thus protecting it even before it has left the secure boundaries of SAP. For more information on Halocore, visit `http://www.secude.com/solutions/halocore/for-sap-netweaver/`.

Summary

The important part in this chapter was to understand the powerful extension of a Dynamic Access Control scenario with integrated AD RMS. Now, you can identify and describe the architecture and components of an AD RMS solution. Obviously, this short chapter about AD RMS doesn't explain the whole technology, but gives you a short starter to work with. In addition, you have learned to describe and configure the Rights Protected Folder solution and protect information based on classification. Next, we will extend our Dynamic Access Control solution.

7
Extending the DAC Base Solution

After applying **Active Directory Rights Management Services** (**AD RMS**) protection to our solution, this chapter will give you an overview about how to extend your base DAC solution and about the available third-party solution vendors. A special topic in this chapter will be the usage of DAC in a **Bring Your Own Device** (**BYOD**) solution. This chapter will cover the following topics:

- Keeping Active Directory attributes up-to-date
- Dynamic Access Control third-party tools
- Use DAC in SharePoint
- BYOD: Using Dynamic Access Control

By the end of this chapter you will have a toolbox of third-party DAC extensions at your disposal, and you should be able to support a BYOD strategy.

Keeping Active Directory attributes up-to-date

A very important aspect in a DAC environment is to keep the attributes in Active Directory up-to-date. For example, if an employee named Jeff Dunham moves from the Legal department to the Finance department, he needs completely different permissions to do his job. On the other hand, if he moves from Zurich to Dubai, he will have other regulations that will have to be applied to the files he works on. Another reason can be that he changes his job role as the manager of the department. For all this information, the best way is to build standards, and drop-down menus are used to define these attributes in the Active Directory application.

Be very careful while exporting files, and sanitize and double-check them before you export them to Active Directory. Wait! In addition, think about an **Identity Management System** to handle these tasks for you automatically day-by-day. If an Identity Management System is too expensive for your organization, you can use the following tools to help you with the task of maintaining a high data quality in your Active Directory:

- ADfind (`http://www.joeware.net/freetools/tools/adfind/`)
- Power Shell native or the Quest PowerGui (`http://powergui.org/index.jspa`)
- Solarwinds AD admin tools (`http://www.solarwinds.com/products/freetools/`)
- Windows Sysinternals suite (`http://technet.microsoft.com/en-us/sysinternals/`)
- Dameware AD Management Tools (`http://www.dameware.com/products/remote-support/product-features/active-directory-management-tools.aspx`)
- LDAP Administrator commercial (`http://www.ldapbrowser.com/`)

Many more tools are available; feel free to use your own set.

Third-party tools for Dynamic Access Control

In the actual market, you will find many Dynamic Access Control additions from third-party vendors to fill the gaps that we still have with Windows 2012 and the 2012 R2 version. This section will just give you an overview about the areas in which different vendors can support you with helpful tools. The list can never be complete; please keep that in mind.

Classification

For classification, **Dataglobal** provides you with some powerful features that include:

- Simplifying the cooperation between business departments with special training sets
- Providing solutions if your criteria has not been defined clearly enough
- Safe and smooth reduction of rule sets

- Metadata-based classification for a good classification performance
- Machine learning for better results and usage of imprecise criteria
- Simulations and tests for quality assurance
- Pattern matching
- Additional special classifiers that can be optionally integrated

Here is an example for the classification of data into **Contracts**, **Logs**, and **Specifications**:

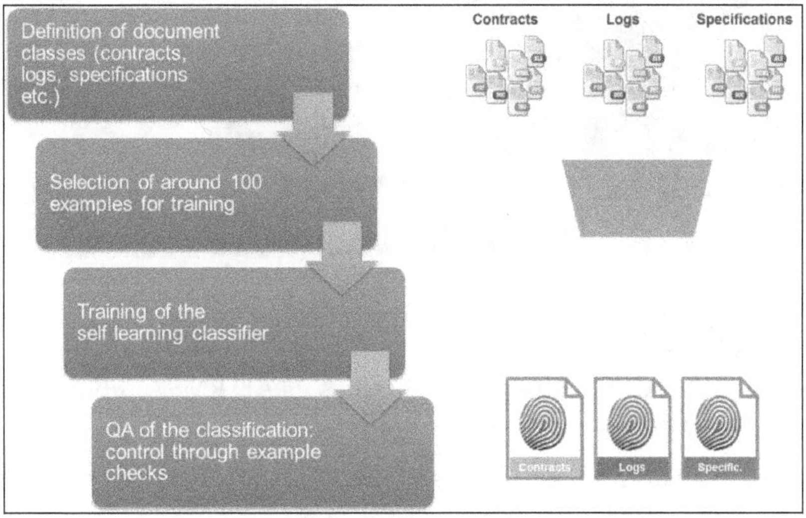

Central Access Policy

For the lifecycle management of Central Access Policies, **NextLabs** provides a **Control Center Policy Studio** with the following main features:

- Central Access Policy lifecycle management
- Dynamic Access Control for Microsoft SharePoint
- Compliance Policy accelerators

The following figure illustrates the policy:

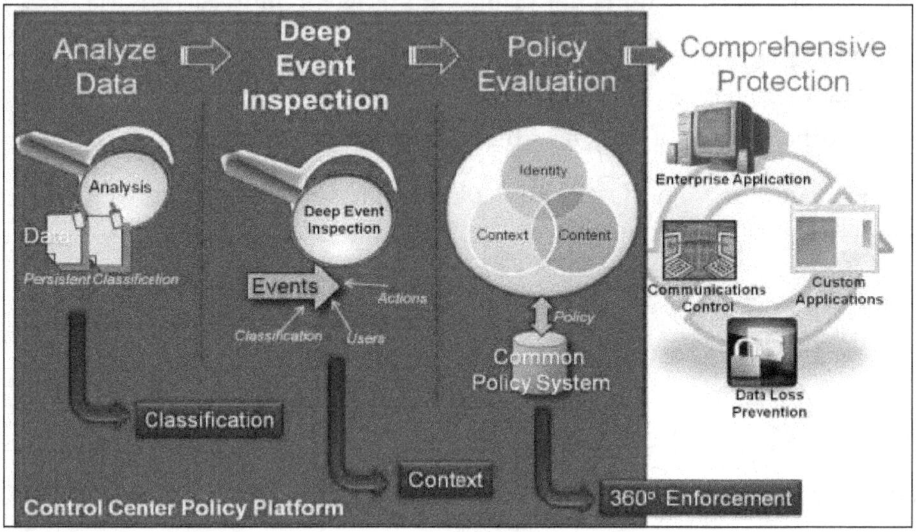

RMS Protection

For integrating with AD RMS, **GigaTrust** extends its AD RMS solutions with Dynamic Access Control as follows:

1. Configure your Dynamic Access Control environment (user claims, resource properties, and central access policies).
2. With the standard behavior of Dynamic Access Control policies, secure your information based on properties and claims.
3. **File Classification Infrastructure** (**FCI**) invokes the Dynamic Policy Protector to RMS, thus protecting access with Policy and Resource Properties captured in the Issuance License.
4. The AD RMS user license will be returned only if the dynamic policy is satisfied by user claims.

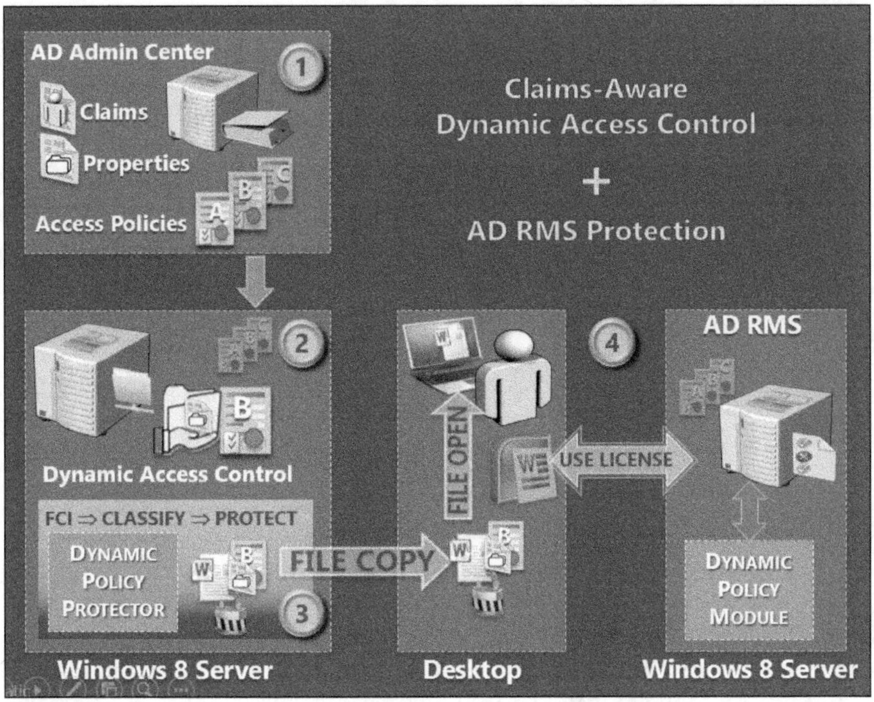

Auditing

JiJi AuditReporter helps you manage auditing with a web-based solution that brings benefits, which you can find at `http://www.jijitechnologies.com/dynamic-access-control-effective-permission-report.aspx`.

They have also provided a video to show the complete functions at `http://www.jijitechnologies.com/dynamic-access-control-video.aspx`.

To see the claims in effective access evaluation, Dynamic Access Control enables information governance with new capabilities for centrally controlling the access and auditing the access to the information in the files. Dynamic Access Control and the Central Access Policies use Active Directory attributes as claims to provide a powerful solution for controlling access and auditing.

With the JiJi AuditReporter, you get the possibility to evaluate the claims that are defined in Dynamic Access Control, and in particular, the Central Access Policies with existing security and share permissions to generate a very useful, resultant access-permission report, as shown in the following screenshot:

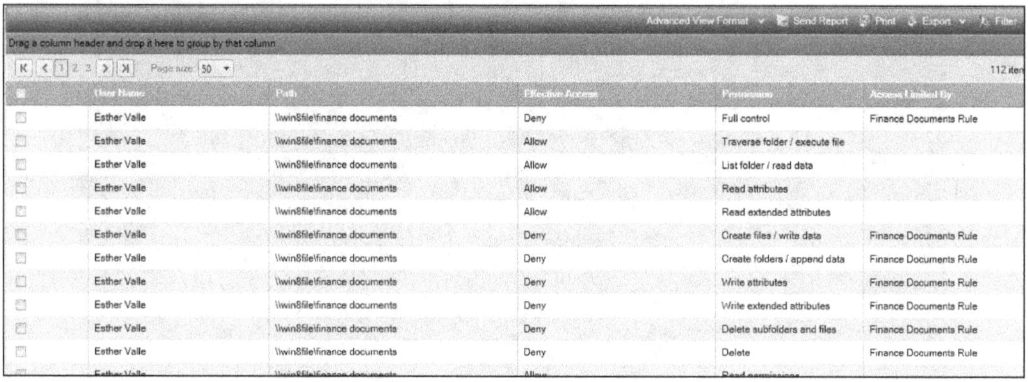

User Name	Path	Effective Access	Permission	Access Limited By
Esther Valle	\\win8file\finance documents	Deny	Full control	Finance Documents Rule
Esther Valle	\\win8file\finance documents	Allow	Traverse folder / execute file	
Esther Valle	\\win8file\finance documents	Allow	List folder / read data	
Esther Valle	\\win8file\finance documents	Allow	Read attributes	
Esther Valle	\\win8file\finance documents	Allow	Read extended attributes	
Esther Valle	\\win8file\finance documents	Deny	Create files / write data	Finance Documents Rule
Esther Valle	\\win8file\finance documents	Deny	Create folders / append data	Finance Documents Rule
Esther Valle	\\win8file\finance documents	Deny	Write attributes	Finance Documents Rule
Esther Valle	\\win8file\finance documents	Deny	Write extended attributes	Finance Documents Rule
Esther Valle	\\win8file\finance documents	Deny	Delete subfolders and files	Finance Documents Rule
Esther Valle	\\win8file\finance documents	Deny	Delete	Finance Documents Rule

Using DAC in SharePoint

Microsoft SharePoint is probably the most popular way to share files today. **TITUS** is working to provide the ability to apply Dynamic Access Control to SharePoint with metadata security for SharePoint (`http://www.titus.com/software/sharepoint/metadata.php`).

The following figure shows an overview of the TITUS solution for SharePoint. See more information about this example at `http://www.titus.com/titus-blog/2012/06/applying-windows-server-2012-dynamic-access-control-to-sharepoint/`.

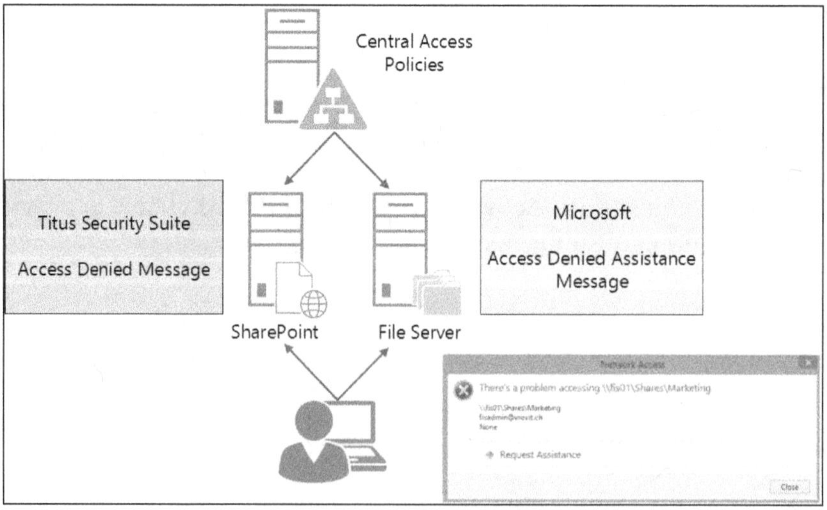

This section provides just a small list of different vendors that can help you to choose the tools to complete your solution.

> Always have a look at the whole suites or portfolios of these vendors because most vendors provide features that other vendors provide as well. Mixing products can be quite a heavy task for most IT departments.

BYOD – using Dynamic Access Control

To support **Bring Your Own Device** (**BYOD**) strategies with information protection is a common need in actual projects. A very good example showing that you can support your BYOD strategy with Dynamic Access Control is the file server feature called **Windows Server 2012 R2 Work Folders**, which allows us to synchronize files directly with our file server. Additionally, Windows Server 2012 R2 Workplace provides us with the possibility of joining different devices such as Windows 8 RT and Apple in a workplace using the device ID to extend the authentication capabilities for claim-based scenarios.

You can find more information about this feature at `http://technet.microsoft.com/en-us/library/dn280945.aspx`.

With the **Work Folders** feature set, you can deploy the following device policies regarding how the information gets stored on the mobile device:

- Encrypt files on the device
- Automatically lock screen and request a password

The following screenshot illustrates the Work Folders feature integrated in the Dynamic Access Control scenario with AD RMS tasks for HBI files applied on the Finance department share:

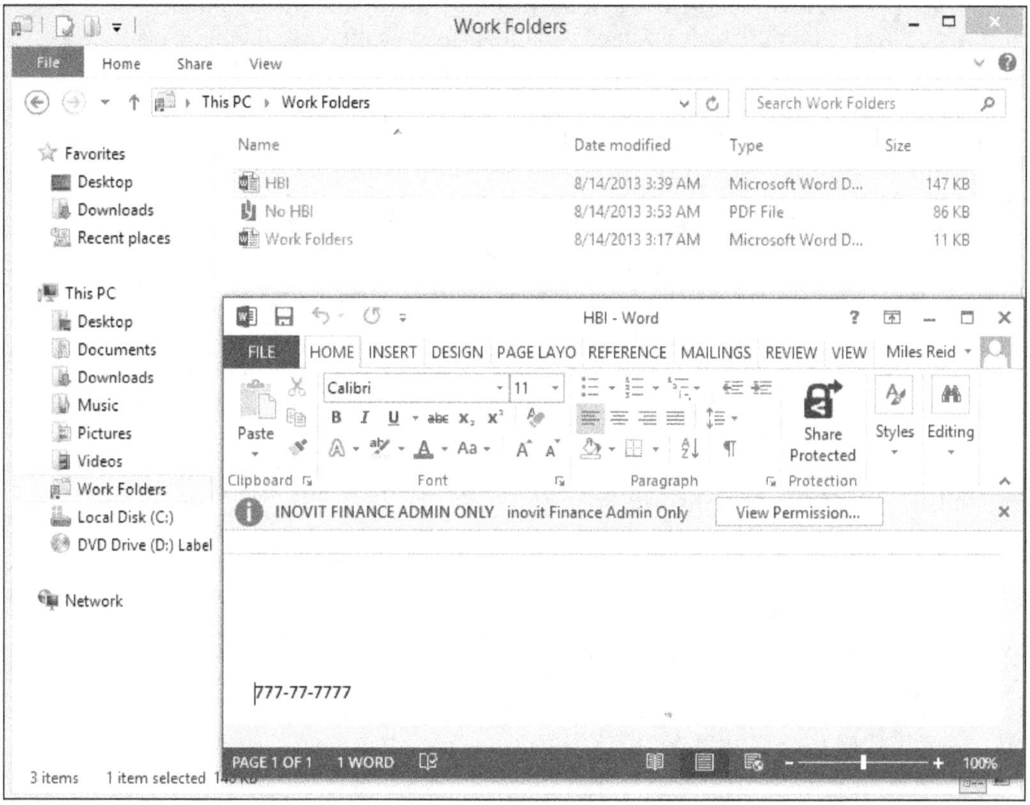

To configure this scenario, you just need to install the Work Folder feature as follows:

1. Go to **Server Manager** on FIS01.
2. Use **Add Roles and Features Wizard** to install the feature.
3. Follow the wizard and click on **Work Folders** under **File and Storage Services | File and iSCSI Services**.
4. Launch **New Sync Share Wizard** from **Server Manager**.
5. Enter the local path where you want to create user folders under the Finance department share.

6. On CLI01, add the following registry keys to avoid conflicts with certificates:
   - `Reg add HKLM\SOFTWARE\Microsoft\Windows\CurrentVersion\WorkFolders /v AllowUnsecureConnection /t REG_DWORD /d 1`
   - `Reg add HKCU\Software\Microsoft\Windows\CurrentVersion\WorkFolders /v ServerUrl /t REG_SZ /d http://fis01.inovit.ch`
   - `Reg add HKLM\SOFTWARE\Microsoft\Windows\CurrentVersion\WorkFolders /v PollingInterval /t REG_DWORD /d 1`
7. Configure your Work Folder on the client, and once that is done, the **Control Panel** will display the status, as shown in the following screenshot:

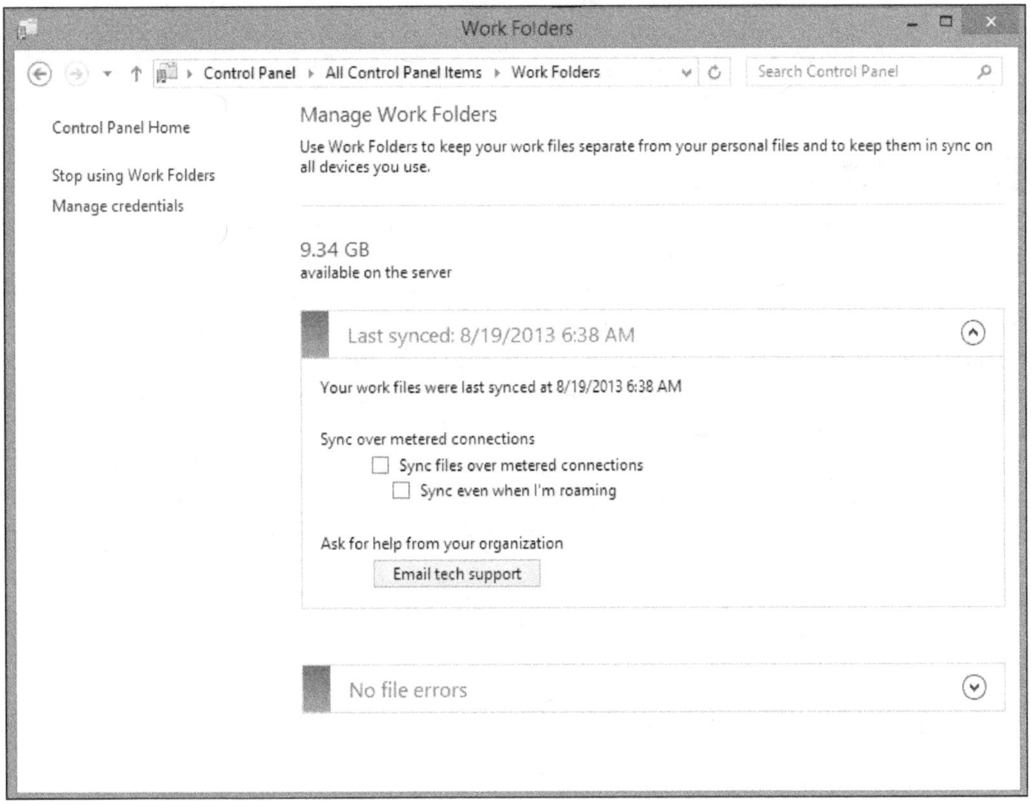

Further information about Work Folders can be found at `http://blogs.technet.com/b/filecab/archive/2013/07/10/introducing-work-folders-on-windows-server-2012-r2.aspx`.

> If you want to include certificates to define whether you have come from a managed or unmanaged device, take a closer look at the authentication assurance mechanism, which has existed since Windows Server 2008 R2 (`http://blogs.technet.com/b/activedirectoryua/archive/2008/11/21/authentication-mechanism-assurance-in-windows-server-2008-r2.aspx`).

In addition, you should configure the claims transformation policy as shown in the following guide to get more experience on how Dynamic Access Control works across organizational boundaries:

`http://technet.microsoft.com/en-us/library/hh831742.aspx`

For this task, you need to extend the lab with an additional domain controller of another forest such as `leano.ch`, and set up a forest trust between them.

Summary

In this chapter we briefly discussed keeping your Active Directory attributes correct and up-to-date for using them with Dynamic Access Control. We also discussed a list of a few third-party tools that can help to extend your implementation and fill the gaps that still exist. Another important information is that the solution is not limited to file servers only. With the TITUS product, you are able to use your attribute-based access control with SharePoint. Also remember that your business can be located anywhere and your solution should include the BYOD point of view. In complex Active Directory structures, for example, in a multi-forest environment, try to work with claim-transformation policies to get a good and solid knowledge on these configurations. In the next chapter we will dive in the automation mechanisms to reduce administrative efforts.

8

Automating the Solution

This chapter will discuss the automation possibilities for this technology. It will give you an idea of different architectures to fulfil the different requirements in actual projects. In particular, we will explain some Microsoft products to reach our goals. In this chapter, we will cover the following topics:

- How to identify the complete solution
- How other Microsoft products can assist you
- Advanced architectures for Information Protection

In this chapter, we'll be using **Dynamic Access Control** (**DAC**) for Information Protection. Equipped and prepared with some ideas, you are ready to go.

Identifying the complete solution

DAC is not only a single feature to protect information from unauthorized access, but also a part of a complete information-protection strategy from Microsoft. The perfect thing is that Microsoft now provides not just a product like in the times of Windows Server 2003, but a complete solution that every product mostly integrates with, along with the availability of a management platform as well.

So let's first start with an easy way to implement an example to automate the `Active Directory` attributes by filling and updating the process from an HR export file you receive from the HR system in the comma-separated value (CSV) format:

1. Double-check and sanitize the export file you received.
2. Build up a PowerShell solution as follows:

```
Import-Module ActiveDirectory

$UserImport = Import-CSV c:\staging\users.csv

$UserImport | Foreach{

Get-ADUser -filter {name -eq $_.name}|Set-ADUSer -TelephoneNumber
$_.TelephoneNumber $_.TelephoneNumber -MobilePhone $_.MobilePhone
-StreetAddress $_.StreetAddress -City $_.City -Title $_.Title}
```

3. Run the script after you are sure that the export file consists of the correct information.
4. You can extend the solution with an error-logging section and a framework to use the scheduled tasks if a new checked file exists in the staging directory.

> Some helpful links to start with this solution are as follows:
>
> - `http://technet.microsoft.com/en-us/library/dd391908%28v=ws.10%29.aspx`
> - `http://technet.microsoft.com/en-us/library/ee617215`
> - `http://technet.microsoft.com/en-us/library/cc748993.aspx`
> - `http://technet.microsoft.com/en-us/library/ff730955.aspx`

The next solution we present in this book covers information protection architecture and will not be completely explained, because capturing all the features of every product will be beyond the scope of this book.

Focused on DAC, we will explain the most important features to automate and manage an information-protection environment. The main components of the solution are as follows:

- Active Directory Services, the Identity Manager, and the System Center Suite
- The HR system
- File Services and the Security tools

The following figure illustrates the architecture, the main components, and the most important relations between the systems:

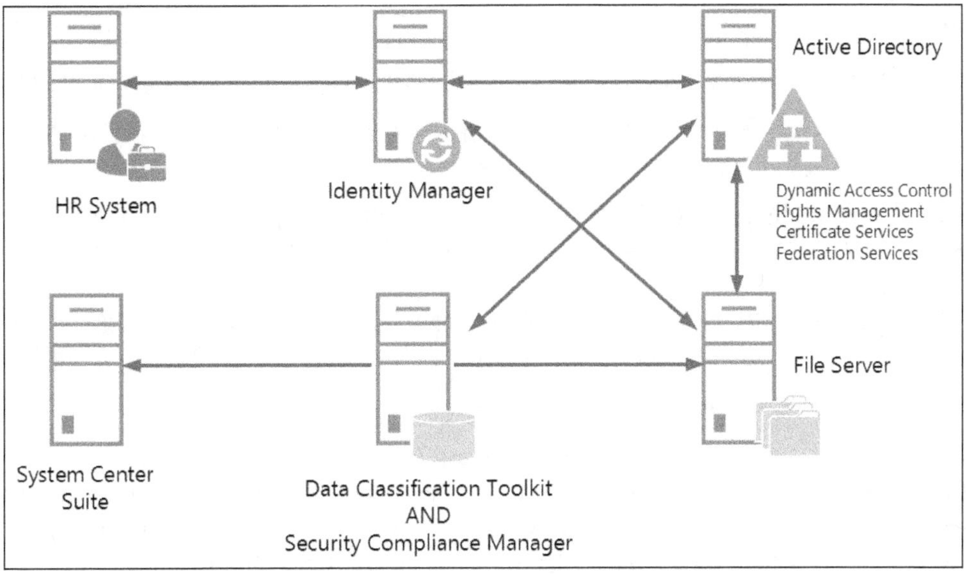

How other Microsoft products can assist you

The **Forefront Identity Manager 2010 R2 (FIM)** plays a main role in an information-protection environment, particularly for integrating DAC. As you already know, DAC defines access to resources based on the `Active Directory` attributes, so it is very important to provide a controlled way to fill attributes with the proper and correct information. The solution we discussed before will act as the foundation for the next solution. Connecting the HR system to the Identity Manager brings many positive effects to a company; for example, you don't need to manage the data several times and you can use the information for building groups and group memberships. Humans work in the HR department as well, and mistakes happen everywhere, but with an Identity Management between HR and `Active Directory`, you are able to control the flow of the attributes to `Active Directory`. Another important point is the group management itself; you cannot go without groups—it is not possible. The Forefront Identity Manager offers a complete Group Management solution that helps you to manage the objects automatically, with a self-service portal and integration in the Office suite. With the integration of **BHOLD suite** in the Identity Manager, you are also able to provide a complete RBAC solution and Compliance and Attestation tools.

> You can read more about the concepts of the BHOLD suite at: `http://technet.microsoft.com/en-us/library/jj134102(v=ws.10).aspx`

Let's start with the main components and tasks. Firstly, you need to start with FIM:

1. Install the FIM 2010 R2 Synchronization Service. Refer to `http://technet.microsoft.com/en-us/library/hh552730(v=ws.10).aspx`.
2. Use the FIM QuickStart Tool to configure your base environment. Refer to `http://technet.microsoft.com/en-us/library/jj134297(v=ws.10).aspx`.
3. Build up a file-based management agent. Refer to `http://technet.microsoft.com/en-us/library/jj572792%28v=ws.10%29.aspx`.
4. Synchronize your HR export file with `Active Directory`.

The `Active Directory` services alone help you to protect your information in different usage scenarios. In the time of **Bring your own device** and the cloud solution, we need to protect sensitive information everywhere and every time. The **Active Directory Certificate Services** provides you with a way to automatically assign certificates for authentication, authorization, and encryption. With Windows 2012/R2, **Windows Intune**, and the **System Center suite**, you are able to distribute and manage certificates sooner in every scenario where you're needed to provide them.

> In DAC, you can also integrate certificates in the expression-based access rules.

Consider, for example, a situation where you need to create certificate-based claim types when you want to use smartcard logon claims for authorization decisions. For example, consider the following attributes along with their values:

Name: `Department and Smart Card Logon`

Access: `Authenticated Users` (this can be changed)

Condition: `@user.department==@resource.department && user.sclogon==yes`

The combination of AD RMS and FCI gives you a very flexible and automatic way to protect your information on your file server. You get a toolset that allows you to protect your information based on your classification rules, and the data can be securely moved to different ways.

> You can find some additional information at:
> `http://technet.microsoft.com/en-us/library/ff625714%28v=ws.10%29.aspx`

In `Active Directory`, you can delegate the `Active Directory` tasks that you control to those who have access, and can modify information for DAC. Be aware that for a working scenario, you need to define strict rule sets for managing attributes.

For example, you could configure the following groups:

- DAC Claim Administrators
- DAC Resource Property Administrators
- DAC Central Access Rule Administrators
- DAC Central Access Policy Administrators

To delegate the permissions, you will find the relevant containers in `Active Directory` by opening `adsiedit.msc` and then browse to **Configuration Partition** | **System** | **Services** | **Claims configuration**.

You will find the following containers to delegate permissions:

- Claim Types
- Resource Properties
- Central Access Rules
- Central Access Policies

The **Data Classification Toolkit** is one of the basic components that helps you to classify your information in a very effective manner based on the experience that applies to actual regulatory and industrial standards. As we discussed in the relevant chapters, you can work with a staging scenario and distribute the tested and actual settings to every file server in your environment.

> For more information about DCT, visit
> `http://technet.microsoft.com/en-us/library/hh204743.aspx.`

Advanced architectures for Information Protection

To get in an advanced information protection scenario, we go to Governance, Risk, and Compliance (GRC) Management. Therefore, Microsoft provides us with the **Security Compliance Manager** and the **System Center suite** that help you to close the circle of managing information protection. Of course, all the other products such as Exchange or SharePoint do their work to close the gaps in this area. These tools support you in the following main areas:

- Defining and deploying security policies
- Collecting and analyzing audit information
- Controlling and managing security configurations
- Integrating into the service management
- Automating and controlling system configurations
- Providing a self-service functionality

The following figure gives you an idea about the different aspects to extend the information protection solution with such products:

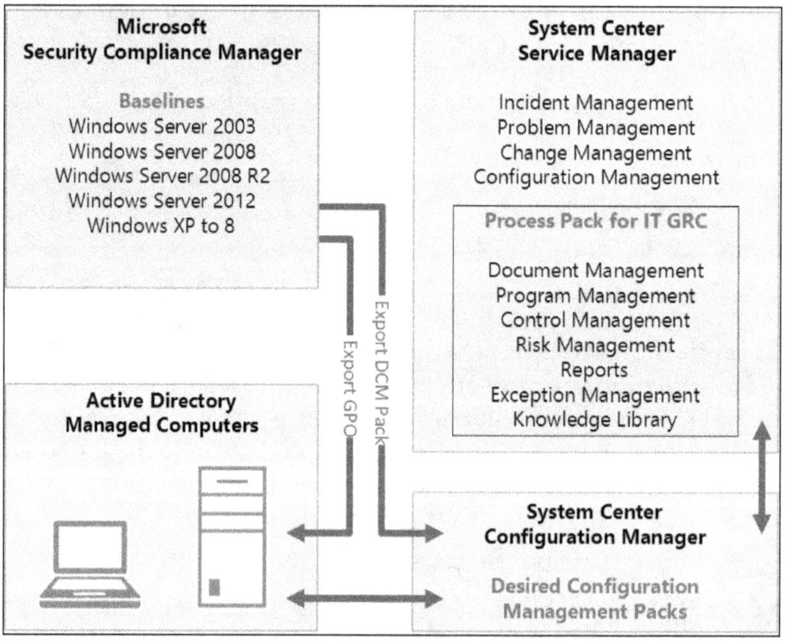

(Source: Microsoft)

[For more information about the Security Compliance Manager, visit `http://technet.microsoft.com/en-us/library/cc677002.aspx`.]

Another important topic is how all these information-protection features work on-premises, in the cloud services, or with business-partner interaction. Consider the following figure which shows different architectures:

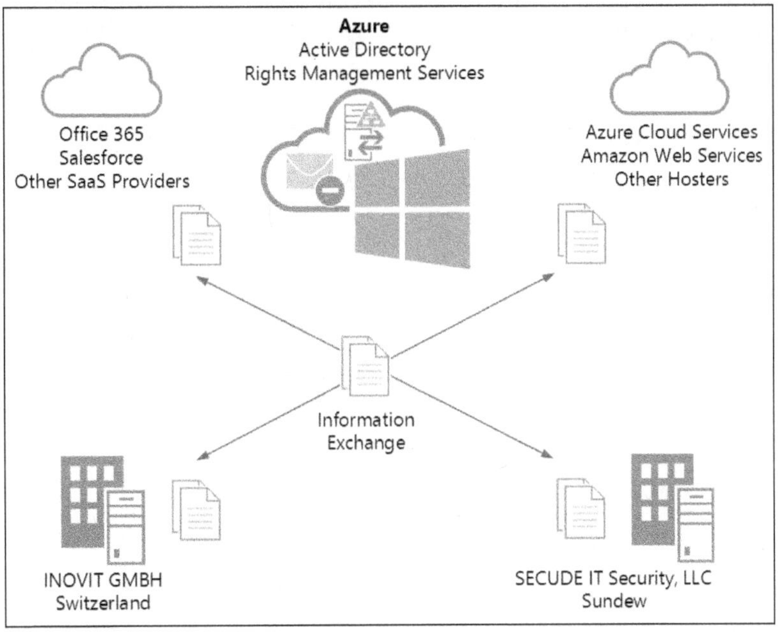

(Source: Microsoft)

The preceding figure illustrates the different scenarios and should give you some ideas about the requirements in your next projects.

Classification is an important task that you need to handle. It is one of the most relevant parts a company needs to think about before using public cloud services, because the knowledge of which information can be stored in the cloud or needs to be secured to be there helps organizations to use more efficient information technology infrastructures.

Summary

After reading this chapter, you should have an idea about the different components in an information protection strategy and which components are essential in an information protection strategy. Also, you should be able to explain how other Microsoft technologies can help you to implement a DAC solution in modules as well as with GRC requirements. Furthermore, you should have an idea about which important facts need to be covered in an information protection project. Next, we will see some common misconfigurations and helpful information for troubleshooting your DAC environment.

9
Troubleshooting

In our final chapter, we will discuss common problems and how they can be addressed. This chapter will give you a tutorial on troubleshooting strategies around Dynamic Access Control that range from general to advanced. It will also offer links to a collection of external resources such as blogs, wikis, and articles. In this chapter we'll be covering the following topics:

- Common misconfigurations
- General troubleshooting
- Advanced troubleshooting

At the end of this chapter, you will have all the relevant information about Dynamic Access Control in your hands. With all the theoretical and practical stuff at your disposal, you can start using this interesting and wonderful technology.

Common misconfigurations

Common misconfiguration issues regarding Central Access Policy include:

- Wrong security filtering settings in the Group Policies
- Missing membership of one or more Central Access Rules
- Group policy object containing the Central Access Policy object does not apply to the file server
- Broken or latent Active Directory and/or SYSVOL replication and connection
- Misconfigured conditional expressions
- The Target Resources condition in a Central Access Rule evaluates to false
- Misconfigured claim information in Active Directory

- Pipeline URLs not accessible from the AD RMS client computer
- Active Directory users with no e-mail address configured
- Incorrect Internet Explorer settings, missing local intranet configuration

General troubleshooting

In this section, we will describe the basic troubleshooting tasks to solve the most common problems that we encounter in Dynamic Access Control.

Domain Controller count

In projects, the first question we get is about the number of Domain Controllers we need to handle the new Kerberos requests with claims information. The best way to determine whether there are enough Domain Controllers is to use performance monitoring counters.

The most relevant performance monitoring counters are:

- Security system-wide statistics \ KDC AS requests
- Security system-wide statistics \ KDC AS requests with claims
- Security system-wide statistics \ KDC AS requests with FAST
- Security system-wide statistics \ KDC S4U2Self requests with claims
- Security system-wide statistics \ KDC TGS requests
- Security system-wide statistics \ KDC TGS requests with FAST

To plan your Domain Controller environment you should adhere to the general recommendations mentioned in the following list and capture the necessary information:

- Windows Server 2003 Domain Controllers:
    - NTDS\KDC AS requests
    - NTDS\KDC TGS requests
- Windows Server 2008 and R2 Domain Controllers:
    - Security system-wide statistics \ KDC AS Requests
    - Security system-wide statistics \ KDC TGS Requests

- Implement Windows Server 2012/R2 Domain Controllers and capture:
    - Security system-wide statistics / KDC AS Requests with claims
    - Security system-side statistics / KDC AS Requests with FAST
    - Security system-wide statistics / KDC TGS Requests with FAST

With the collected information, you will be able to see how many KDC requests are transmitted to the older Domain Controllers, and you can use these numbers to estimate the amount of Windows 2012/R2 Domain Controllers required for your Dynamic Access Control solution.

Data quality of Active Directory attributes

Data quality in Active Directory is also a common problem at the beginning of a project. So, first you should check the availability of the claim information you want to use on the user objects. You can do this in many ways.

For example, you can use the following options to find out whether the `Department` field is set for all the user accounts in the environment:

- For PowerShell, the command is `Get-ADUser -Filter * -Property Department | ft`. The command will produce the following output:

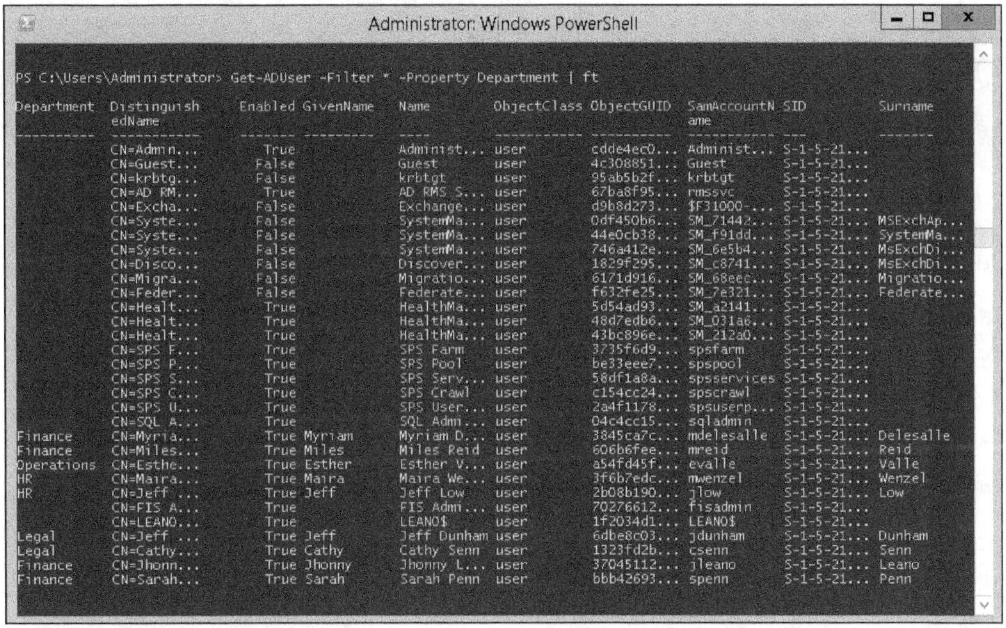

```
Administrator: Windows PowerShell

PS C:\Users\Administrator> Get-ADUser -Filter * -Property Department | ft

Department  Distinguish    Enabled GivenName   Name          ObjectClass ObjectGUID  SamAccountN SID              Surname
            edName                                                                   ame
----------  -----------    ------- ---------   ----          ----------- ----------  ----------- ---              -------
            CN=Admin...       True             Administ...   user        cdde4ec0... Administ... S-1-5-21...
            CN=Guest...      False             Guest         user        4c308851... Guest       S-1-5-21...
            CN=krbtg...      False             krbtgt        user        95ab5b2f... krbtgt      S-1-5-21...
            CN=AD RM...       True             AD RMS S...   user        67ba8f95... rmssvc      S-1-5-21...
            CN=Excha...      False             Exchange...   user        d9b8d273... $F31000-... S-1-5-21...
            CN=Syste...      False             SystemMa...   user        0df450b6... SM_71442... S-1-5-21... MSExchAp...
            CN=Syste...      False             SystemMa...   user        44e0cb38... SM_f91dd... S-1-5-21... SystemMa...
            CN=Syste...      False             SystemMa...   user        746a412e... SM_6e5b4... S-1-5-21... MsExchDi...
            CN=Disco...      False             Discover...   user        1829f295... SM_c8741... S-1-5-21... MsExchDi...
            CN=Migra...      False             Migratio...   user        6171d916... SM_68eec... S-1-5-21... Migratio...
            CN=Feder...      False             Federate...   user        f632fe25... SM_7e321... S-1-5-21... Federate...
            CN=Healt...       True             HealthMa...   user        5d54ad93... SM_a2141... S-1-5-21...
            CN=Healt...       True             HealthMa...   user        48d7edb6... SM_031a6... S-1-5-21...
            CN=Healt...       True             HealthMa...   user        43bc896e... SM_212a0... S-1-5-21...
            CN=SPS F...       True             SPS Farm      user        3735f6d9... spsfarm     S-1-5-21...
            CN=SPS P...       True             SPS Pool      user        be33eee7... spspool     S-1-5-21...
            CN=SPS S...       True             SPS Serv...   user        58df1a8a... spsservices S-1-5-21...
            CN=SPS C...       True             SPS Crawl     user        c154cc24... spscrawl    S-1-5-21...
            CN=SPS U...       True             SPS User...   user        2a4f1178... spsuserp... S-1-5-21...
            CN=SQL A...       True             SQL Admi...   user        04c4cc15... sqladmin    S-1-5-21...
Finance     CN=Myria...       True Myriam      Myriam D...   user        3845ca7c... mdelesalle  S-1-5-21... Delesalle
Finance     CN=Miles...       True Miles       Miles Reid    user        606b6fee... mreid       S-1-5-21... Reid
Operations  CN=Esthe...       True Esther      Esther V...   user        a54fd45f... evalle      S-1-5-21... Valle
HR          CN=Maira...       True Maira       Maira We...   user        3f6b7edc... mwenzel     S-1-5-21... Wenzel
HR          CN=Jeff ...       True Jeff        Jeff Low      user        2b08b190... jlow        S-1-5-21... Low
            CN=FIS A...       True             FIS Admi...   user        70276612... fisadmin    S-1-5-21...
            CN=LEANO...       True             LEANO$        user        1f2034d1... LEANO$      S-1-5-21...
Legal       CN=Jeff ...       True Jeff        Jeff Dunham   user        6dbe8c03... jdunham     S-1-5-21... Dunham
Legal       CN=Cathy...       True Cathy       Cathy Senn    user        1323fd2b... csenn       S-1-5-21... Senn
Finance     CN=Jhonn...       True Jhonny      Jhonny L...   user        37045112... jleano      S-1-5-21... Leano
Finance     CN=Sarah...       True Sarah       Sarah Penn    user        bbb42693... spenn       S-1-5-21... Penn
```

For AdFind (`http://www.joeware.net/freetools/tools/adfind/`), the command is `adfind -default -f "&(objectcategory=person)(objectclass=user)(department=*)" name displayname samaccountname -csv > departments.csv`.

> Keep in mind that there is a significant difference between an Active Directory attribute that is not set and an attribute configured with a space value. An attribute configured with a space value can lead you to misconfigured information on claims.

Checking the user and device claims

After checking the data quality in the Active Directory attribute, the correct value for the Active Directory attribute is set to the user or computer for which you need to check the information on claims. To check the user claims, we use the following command:

```
whoami /claims
```

The previous command will produce the following example output:

```
C:\>whoami /claims

USER CLAIMS INFORMATION
-----------------------

Claim Name    Claim ID                                Flags Type   Values
============  ======================================  ===== ====== =======
"country"     ad://ext/country:88d06569cf6cefbf             String "CH"
"department"  ad://ext/department:88d065699dec4651          String "Legal"
```

You can also check the claims, for a given security principal, by using Windows PowerShell and the Windows Identity .NET class library:

```
(New-Object System.Security.Principal.WindowsIdentity
  ("jdunham@inovit.ch")).UserClaims
```

Additionally, if you need to check the group membership, you can use the `whoami` command, which is as follows:

```
whoami /groups /fo list or with | findstr "S-1-5-21-0-0-0-497"
```

You need to take a closer look for the claims valid group, or a group with the security identifier as `S-1-5-21-0-0-0-497`.

You can use the following PowerShell command to find the claims information for a device:

```
$(new-object System.Security.Principal.WindowsIdentity
  ("cli01@inovit.ch"))
```

The previous command will produce the following example output:

```
Copyright (C) 2013 Microsoft Corporation. All rights reserved.

PS C:\> $(new-object System.Security.Principal.WindowsIdentity("cli01@inovit.ch"))


AuthenticationType  :
ImpersonationLevel  : Identification
IsAuthenticated     : True
IsGuest             : False
IsSystem            : False
IsAnonymous         : False
Name                : INOVIT\CLI01$
Owner               : S-1-5-21-857538528-3813495235-3532345341-1109
User                : S-1-5-21-857538528-3813495235-3532345341-1109
Groups              : {S-1-5-21-857538528-3813495235-3532345341-515, S-1-1-0, S-1-5-32-545, S-1-5-2..
Token               : 4032
UserClaims          : {http://schemas.xmlsoap.org/ws/2005/05/identity/claims/name: INOVIT\CLI01$,
                      http://schemas.microsoft.com/ws/2008/06/identity/claims/primarysid:
                      S-1-5-21-857538528-3813495235-3532345341-1109,
                      http://schemas.microsoft.com/ws/2008/06/identity/claims/primarygroupsid:
                      S-1-5-21-857538528-3813495235-3532345341-515,
                      http://schemas.microsoft.com/ws/2008/06/identity/claims/groupsid:
                      S-1-5-21-857538528-3813495235-3532345341-515...}
DeviceClaims        : {}
Claims              : {http://schemas.xmlsoap.org/ws/2005/05/identity/claims/name: INOVIT\CLI01$,
                      http://schemas.microsoft.com/ws/2008/06/identity/claims/primarysid:
                      S-1-5-21-857538528-3813495235-3532345341-1109,
                      http://schemas.microsoft.com/ws/2008/06/identity/claims/primarygroupsid:
                      S-1-5-21-857538528-3813495235-3532345341-515,
                      http://schemas.microsoft.com/ws/2008/06/identity/claims/groupsid:
                      S-1-5-21-857538528-3813495235-3532345341-515...}
Actor               :
BootstrapContext    :
Label               :
NameClaimType       : http://schemas.xmlsoap.org/ws/2005/05/identity/claims/name
RoleClaimType       : http://schemas.microsoft.com/ws/2008/06/identity/claims/groupsid
```

Domain connectivity

To apply Group Policies, resolve user accounts, and so on, you need connectivity to a Domain Controller in your environment. The `nltest /sc_query:inovit.ch` command allows you to check the connectivity and a `NERR_Success` message is expected for valid connectivity, as shown in the following screenshot:

```
PS C:\> nltest /sc_query:inovit.ch
Flags: 30 HAS_IP  HAS_TIMESERV
Trusted DC Name \\ADS01.inovit.ch
Trusted DC Connection Status Status = 0 0x0 NERR_Success
The command completed successfully
PS C:\> _
```

Advanced Security Editor

In order to use graphical user interfaces to work on Dynamic Access Control problems, we need a functioning Domain Controller connectivity and service availability. To use Kerberos, the **Effective Access** and **Share** tabs in **Advanced Security Settings** require a connection to the remote server. You can use the following `klist` command to check this connectivity and see the actual Kerberos tickets:

```
klist tickets
```

To verify if a ticket exists, check the following:

- The `Client` portion of the ticket contains the principal name of the current user
- The `Server` portion of the ticket reports the **Service Principal Name** (**SPN**) with the prefix, `cifs/`, followed by a fully qualified computer name, as shown in the following screenshot:

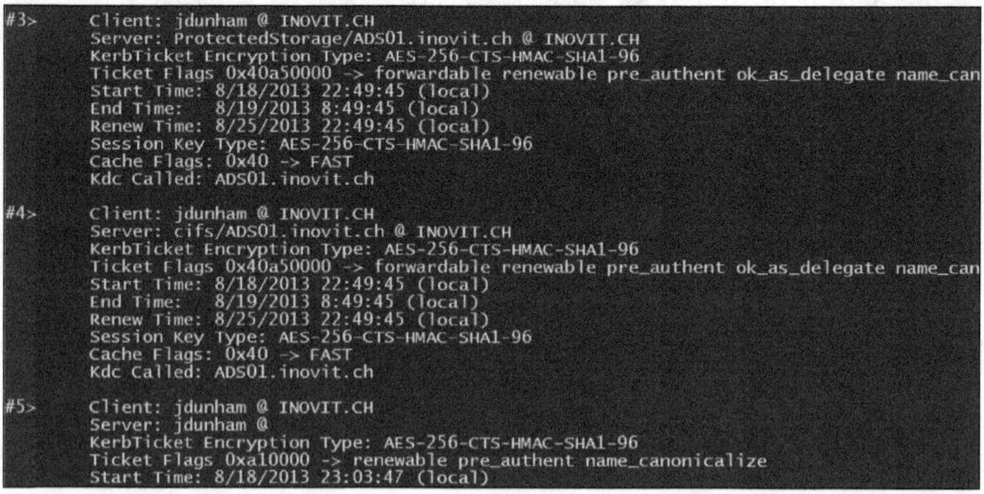
#3>	Client: jdunham @ INOVIT.CH
Server: ProtectedStorage/ADS01.inovit.ch @ INOVIT.CH
KerbTicket Encryption Type: AES-256-CTS-HMAC-SHA1-96
Ticket Flags 0x40a50000 -> forwardable renewable pre_authent ok_as_delegate name_can
Start Time: 8/18/2013 22:49:45 (local)
End Time: 8/19/2013 8:49:45 (local)
Renew Time: 8/25/2013 22:49:45 (local)
Session Key Type: AES-256-CTS-HMAC-SHA1-96
Cache Flags: 0x40 -> FAST
Kdc Called: ADS01.inovit.ch
#4>	Client: jdunham @ INOVIT.CH
Server: cifs/ADS01.inovit.ch @ INOVIT.CH
KerbTicket Encryption Type: AES-256-CTS-HMAC-SHA1-96
Ticket Flags 0x40a50000 -> forwardable renewable pre_authent ok_as_delegate name_can
Start Time: 8/18/2013 22:49:45 (local)
End Time: 8/19/2013 8:49:45 (local)
Renew Time: 8/25/2013 22:49:45 (local)
Session Key Type: AES-256-CTS-HMAC-SHA1-96
Cache Flags: 0x40 -> FAST
Kdc Called: ADS01.inovit.ch
#5>	Client: jdunham @ INOVIT.CH
Server: jdunham @
KerbTicket Encryption Type: AES-256-CTS-HMAC-SHA1-96
Ticket Flags 0xa10000 -> renewable pre_authent name_canonicalize
Start Time: 8/18/2013 23:03:47 (local)

Furthermore, the **Share** tab depends on the communication with the file server using the Windows Remote Management RPC:

You can use the `SC \\fis01 query winmgmt` command to get the following output:

```
C:\>SC \\fis01 query winmgmt

SERVICE_NAME: winmgmt
        TYPE               : 20  WIN32_SHARE_PROCESS
        STATE              : 4  RUNNING
                                (STOPPABLE, PAUSABLE, ACCEPTS_SHUTDOWN)
        WIN32_EXIT_CODE    : 0  (0x0)
        SERVICE_EXIT_CODE  : 0  (0x0)
        CHECKPOINT         : 0x0
        WAIT_HINT          : 0x0
```

The order of entries in the Permissions tab

In this section we will list the rules which are to be used while ordering the entries in the **Permissions** tab. The rules for canonical ordering are:

- Explicit Deny type permission entries
- Explicit Allow type permission entries
- Inherited Deny type permission entries from the parent
- Inherited Allow type permission entries from the parent
- Inherited Deny type permission entries from the grandparent
- Inherited Allow type permission entries from the grandparent
- Allow and Deny inheritance continue to traverse upward until they reach the root of the volume

The Central Policy tab

The **Central Policy** tab won't be visible unless the Group Policies are applied to the server. Use the `gpupdate /force` command to force the policy update, and using the `gpresult /R` command, check whether your desired policy is applied.

FCI - resource conditions and resource properties

The **Classification** tab reads the resource property information from Active Directory and caches the information locally. This information is updated every hour. If you cannot see your freshly defined resource properties, refresh the locally cached classification information by using the following command:

```
Update-FsrmClassificationPropertyDefinition
```

You can also force the **Classification** tab to update its local cache, by using the following command:

```
reg delete HKLM\Software\Microsoft\
FileClassificationInfrastructure /v AdLastSync /f
```

If you are not able to see the **Classification** tab in **Windows Explorer**, there are two possible reasons:

- The Desktop Experience Feature is not installed
- The File Server Resource Manager role is not installed

To show this tab on Windows 8 or 8.1 devices, configure the following two Computer Group Policies:

- **File Classification Infrastructure**: The Display Classification tab in File Explorer
- **File Classification Infrastructure**: Specify the list of classification properties

Access Control Lists

To get the current ACL for a share, you can use the `get-acl` PowerShell command:

```
get-acl \\fis01\shares | fl
```

This will produce the following output:

```
PS C:\> get-acl \\fis01\shares\ | fl

Path   : Microsoft.PowerShell.Core\FileSystem::\\fis01\shares\
Owner  : BUILTIN\Administrators
Group  : INOVIT\Domain Users
Access : CREATOR OWNER Allow  FullControl
         NT AUTHORITY\Authenticated Users Allow  ReadAndExecute, Synchronize
         NT AUTHORITY\SYSTEM Allow  FullControl
         BUILTIN\Administrators Allow  FullControl
Audit  :
Sddl   : O:BAG:DUD:PAI(A;OICIIO;FA;;;CO)(A;OICI;0x1200a9;;;AU)(A;OICI;FA;;;SY)(A;OICI;FA;;;E
```

Advanced troubleshooting

We will take a closer look into the **Claim Transformation Policies** (**CTPs**) for troubleshooting because you will work over Active Directory forest boundaries.

Domain function level

First, you need to check your domain function level to be sure you meet the requirements for CTPs by using the following command:

```
(Get-ADDomain).DomainMode
```

The command will produce the following output:

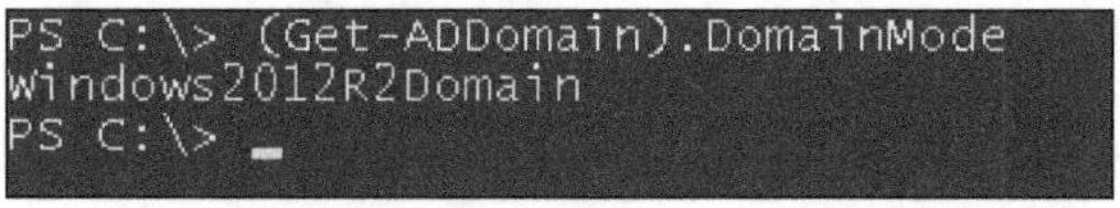

Active Directory trust

Next, we need to check the Active Directory trust between the two forests. You can use the `Get-ADTrust` PowerShell command as shown in the following screenshot:

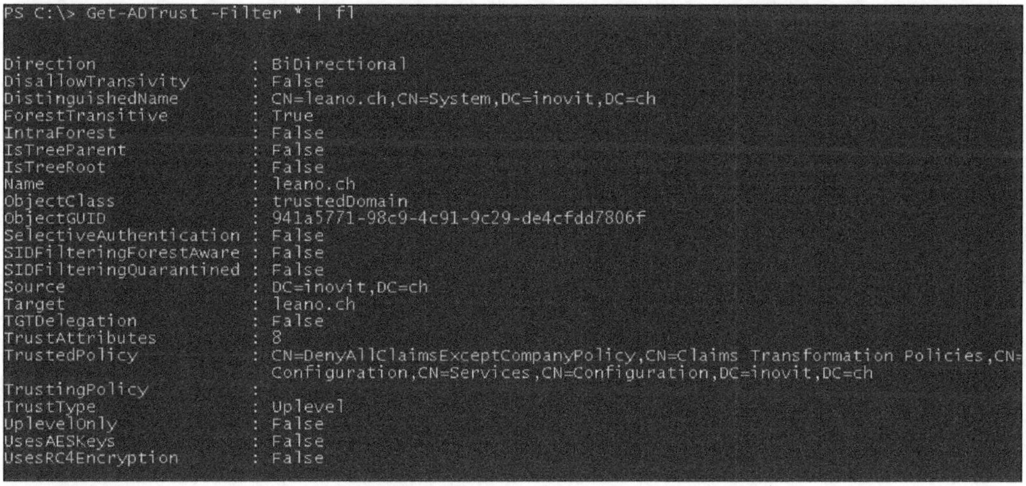

PS C:\> Get-ADTrust -Filter * | fl
Direction : BiDirectional
DisallowTransivity : False
DistinguishedName : CN=leano.ch,CN=System,DC=inovit,DC=ch
ForestTransitive : True
IntraForest : False
IsTreeParent : False
IsTreeRoot : False
Name : leano.ch
ObjectClass : trustedDomain
ObjectGUID : 941a5771-98c9-4c91-9c29-de4cfdd7806f
SelectiveAuthentication : False
SIDFilteringForestAware : False
SIDFilteringQuarantined : False
Source : DC=inovit,DC=ch
Target : leano.ch
TGTDelegation : False
TrustAttributes : 8
TrustedPolicy : CN=DenyAllClaimsExceptCompanyPolicy,CN=Claims Transformation Policies,CN=
Configuration,CN=Services,CN=Configuration,DC=inovit,DC=ch
TrustingPolicy :
TrustType : Uplevel
UplevelOnly : False
UsesAESKeys : False
UsesRC4Encryption : False

Claim Transformation Policy (CTP)

After you check the trust between the both forests, we will take a closer look at the CTPs themselves by using the following command:

```
Get-ADClaimTransformPolicy -Filter *
```

In our example, the policy limits claims to the company claim.

The following directory services event logs help you to identify problems:

```
Event IDs 2923, 2924, 2925, 2926, or 2950
```

These events indicate that the claims transformation engine drops claims if there is a problem with the transformation rule or policy.

Summary

After going through this chapter, you should be able to troubleshoot the most common problems in a Dynamic Access Control scenario. The samples mentioned in this chapter comprise only a small portion of the many troubleshooting tips available. So go ahead and read the Dynamic Access troubleshooting guide available at `http://www.microsoft.com/en-us/download/details.aspx?id=36830`.

Index

A

B

C

D

E

F

U

V

W

PACKT PUBLISHING enterprise
professional expertise distilled

Thank you for buying
Learning Microsoft Windows Server 2012
Dynamic Access Control

About Packt Publishing

Packt, pronounced 'packed', published its first book "Mastering phpMyAdmin for Effective MySQL Management" in April 2004 and subsequently continued to specialize in publishing highly focused books on specific technologies and solutions.

Our books and publications share the experiences of your fellow IT professionals in adapting and customizing today's systems, applications, and frameworks. Our solution based books give you the knowledge and power to customize the software and technologies you're using to get the job done. Packt books are more specific and less general than the IT books you have seen in the past. Our unique business model allows us to bring you more focused information, giving you more of what you need to know, and less of what you don't.

Packt is a modern, yet unique publishing company, which focuses on producing quality, cutting-edge books for communities of developers, administrators, and newbies alike. For more information, please visit our website: `www.packtpub.com`.

About Packt Enterprise

In 2010, Packt launched two new brands, Packt Enterprise and Packt Open Source, in order to continue its focus on specialization. This book is part of the Packt Enterprise brand, home to books published on enterprise software - software created by major vendors, including (but not limited to) IBM, Microsoft and Oracle, often for use in other corporations. Its titles will offer information relevant to a range of users of this software, including administrators, developers, architects, and end users.

Writing for Packt

We welcome all inquiries from people who are interested in authoring. Book proposals should be sent to author@packtpub.com. If your book idea is still at an early stage and you would like to discuss it first before writing a formal book proposal, contact us; one of our commissioning editors will get in touch with you.

We're not just looking for published authors; if you have strong technical skills but no writing experience, our experienced editors can help you develop a writing career, or simply get some additional reward for your expertise.

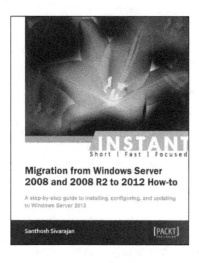

www.ingramcontent.com/pod-product-compliance
Lightning Source LLC
LaVergne TN
LVHW081345050326
832903LV00024B/1332
* 9 7 8 1 7 8 2 1 7 8 1 8 7 *